Cross-Stitch a Beautiful Christmas

Cross-Stitch a Beautiful Christmas

Jutta Lammèr

Sterling Publishing Co., Inc. New York

Translated by Elisabeth E. Reinersmann
Drawings by Ekkehard Dreschel
Photographs by Thomas A. Weiss
Edited by Barbara Busch

Library of Congress Cataloging-in-Publication Data

Lammèr, Jutta.
[Sticken für Weihnachten. English]
Cross-stitch a beautiful Christmas / by Jutta Lammèr ;
[photography, Thomas Weiss ; drawings, Ekkehard Drechsel].
p. cm.
Translation of: Sticken für Weihnachten.
Includes index.
ISBN 0-8069-8310-8
1. Cross-stitch—Patterns. 2. Christmas decorations. I. Title.
TT778.C76L3713 1990 91-12851
746.44'3041—dc20 CIP

[CIP]

10 9 8 7 6 5 4 3 2 1

Published 1991 by Sterling Publishing Company, Inc.
387 Park Avenue South, New York, N.Y. 10016

Distributed in Canada by Sterling Publishing
% Canadian Manda Group, P.O. Box 920, Station U
Toronto, Ontario, Canada M8Z 5P9
Distributed in Great Britain and Europe by Cassell PLC
Villiers House, 41/47 Strand, London WC2N 5JE
Distributed in Australia by Capricorn Ltd.
P.O. Box 665, Lane Cove, NSW 2066
Printed in Hong Kong

Sterling ISBN 0-8069-8310-8

INTRODUCTION

Although it requires concentration, cross-stitching is one of the most relaxing of all pursuits.

A finished cross-stitching project, however, often looks easier than it actually is, and only those with experience know its degree of difficulty. Beginners, therefore, are well advised not to be too ambitious. For their first project they might want to choose a motif from the sampler on page 59. The border design on pages 20 and 21 can also be used for small, single projects. For those who have just discovered this form of simple needlework, every sampler provided has an estimate of the amount of time needed to finish the project. As with all endeavors, there are those who work rapidly and those who need a bit more time. For some the process itself is the joy, while for others it is the finished project that matters.

The book you hold in your hand presents a wide range of motifs for the Christmas season, including both traditional and modern; some are easy, some more difficult. Each is accompanied by detailed instructions, and whatever your level of expertise there is something to provide you with enjoyment.

TECHNIQUE

Cross-stitching is accomplished by first making an understitch, going from the lower left to the upper right, and then the topstitch, which goes in the opposite direction. It is important that this technique is adhered to for each and every cross-stitch in order to achieve a uniform surface. Always complete one row of understitches in one direction before going on to do the topstitch in the opposite direction. It does not matter if you opt for the up-and-down or the left-to-right method. Just make sure you choose one of the two and stick with it.

Work in horizontal rows, using linen as the base material, carry the embroidery floss from the back to the front between two threads of the material. Then guide the thread diagonally across two "squares." as shown, and carry the embroidery floss from the front to the back of the linen. Continue until the row is finished (see illustration a). Complete the row with the topstitch, working in the opposite direction and using the same holes that were used for the understitch (see illustration b). Care should be taken that each stitch is completed cleanly. This means that while making the stitch, the embroidery needle does not split either the thread of the linen or the embroidery floss already in place. The embroidery floss on the back of your project will run vertically (see the illustration on page 7).

To work the vertical rows, carry the embroidery floss from the back of the material to the front and proceed by guiding it diagonally across two threads of the linen. The floss can then be pulled through to the back of the material and the next step done separately. It is, however, possible to guide the neeedle horizontally underneath two threads of the linen (see illustration c) which would then become the first step for the next stitch. For the topstitch proceed in the same way, but in the opposite direction (see illustration d on this page). The embroidery thread in the back will run horizontally (see the illustration d on page 7).

Make sure that the embroidery floss lies flat and even on the surface and the linen does not pucker up underneath the stitches. The overall appearance of your project will be more pleasing if the understitch is carried out with a bit more tension than the topstitch.

In order to avoid pulling the floss through to the front when starting a new strand, make a loop at the end of the floss rather than a knot. The loop can easily be undone and the end of the floss hidden under the already existing stitches. Most experienced embroiderers make sure that the end of a new strand is positioned parallel to the row that has just been finished. In this way it will be covered automatically during the process of stitching the next row.

Generations of embroidery enthusiasts have used the traditional horizontal method: starting at the bottom row and, row by row working up to the top row. But lately the vertical method has become popular, working from the left to the right side. When making the topstitch, using the vertical method, the needle for each stitch that pulls floss through the linen from front to back is carried out in a free space (see illustration c), while for the stitch that pulls the floss through the linen from back to front the needle is used in the same hole that was used in the previous row (see diagram d).

It is easier to control a needle when stitching through the linen from front to back. It therefore makes sense to start work on the top, when using the vertical method, and at the bottom, when using the horizontal method. This is particularly important when more than one strand of embroidery floss is used in the same hole. It is much easier to make a precise stitch when the needle is guided from the front to the back. Trying to guide a needle from the back to the front is much more difficult. Another advantage: when going from front to back, the embroidery floss can pull a slightly frayed floss from a neighboring stitch down with it. Going from back to front only increases the fraying.

Photos on the opposite page show the difference between the traditional and the newer method: e and f are done horizontally, g and h vertically.

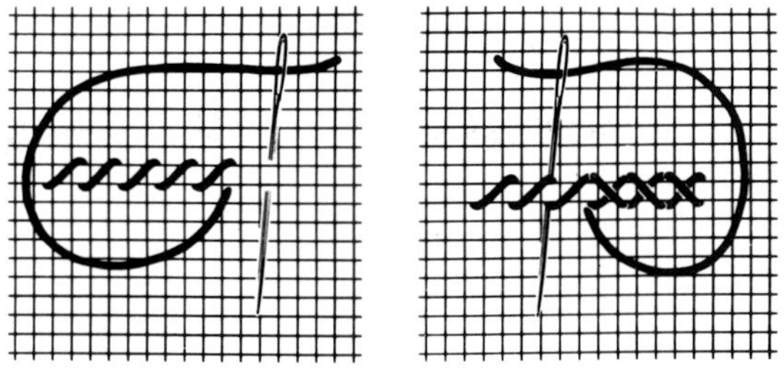

a b

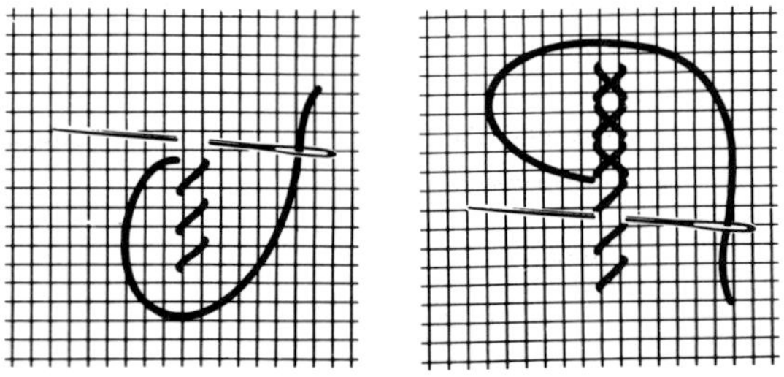

c d

WORKING WITH PATTERNS AND SYMBOLS

Most of the samples in this book are shown on the right-hand pages, with the patterns and list of symbols on the left-hand pages providing the numbers representing the respective colors used for the project (see display on pages 10/11). In cases where it cannot be shown on the left side, a notation is made of where to find it. Each symbol represents one cross-stitch. One cross-stitch is carried out over a square of two threads of the embroidery linen.

Before starting your project, determine the center of the material as well as the center of the pattern. The center is the intersecting point of the vertical and horizontal midline. An accurate center will assure a properly placed motif on the embroidery linen. Counting and transferring a pattern to the linen is not difficult when the motif is small. A small ruler or piece of cardboard is all that is needed to stay in the row you are working on.

For larger projects with many different colors the following suggestions will make the job easier: copy the sampler you have chosen and attach the copy to a piece of Styrofoam (you can obtain from a furniture or appliance store.) Use two pins to mark the end and the beginning of the row you intend to work on. If necessary, use a third pin to mark the point at which you intend to interrupt your work. This eliminates any confusion.

(Please note that in some instances the patterns of the samplers are not always on the same page. If such is the case, the necessary information is given).

EMBROIDERY LINEN

Every sampler in this book has been embroidered on #12-linen. This means that since cross- and backstitches are stitched over two threads, a thread count of 12 gives 6 × 6 cross-stitches. This enables you to determine the size of a finished project. With the exception of border designs for

tablecloth and table runners on pages 20/21, we have provided the measurements for each finished project. However, measurements and thread count may differ from one linen to another. If, for instance, #10.5-linen is used, two threads will accommodate 5¼ cross-stitches and the overall size of the finished project will be larger. The wreaths displayed above show the difference: the wreath on the left was embroidered on linen #10.5; the wreath on the right was embroidered on linen #12.

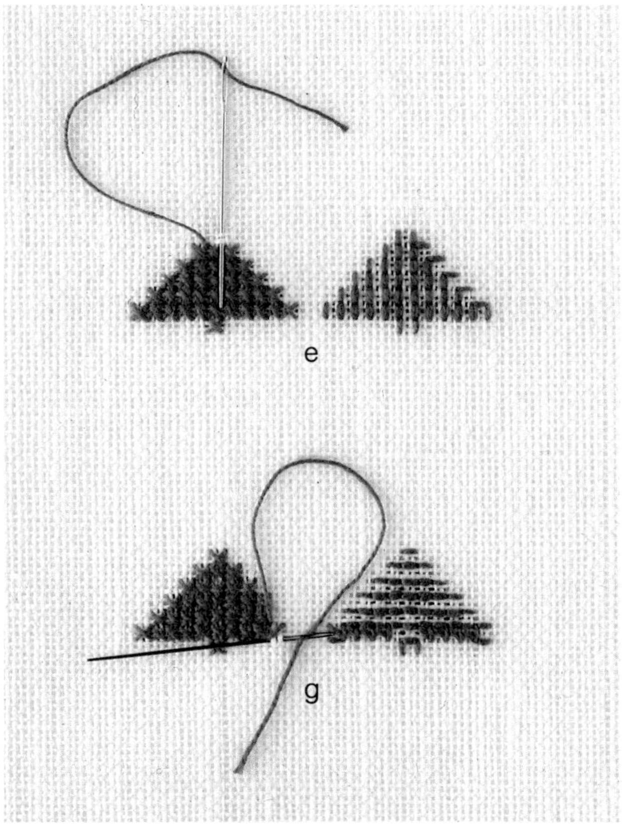

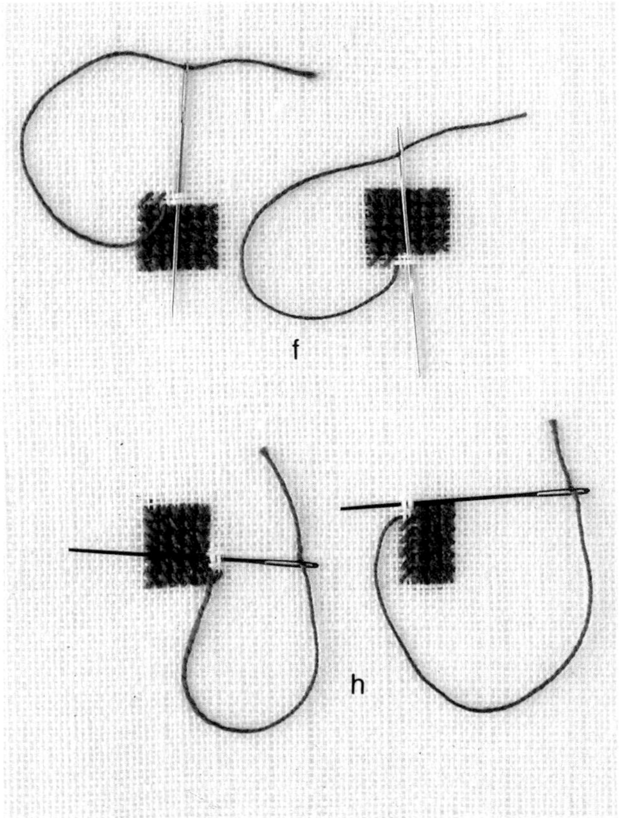

Besides linen, the classical material used in Denmark, other materials are often chosen. The best known is aida-cloth, made specifically for cross-stitch. Only one thread is used for each cross-stitch with these two materials. Single-strand stramin is also used for cross-stitch projects, and, here too, only one strand is used for each cross-stitch. The photos below show four finished projects each embroidered on different materials: upper left on linen #12; upper right on aida-cloth; lower left on practice cloth; lower right on single-strand stramin. With the exception of the upper left sampler (on linen #12), which measures 3,6 cm in height, all projects are 3,1 cm in height.

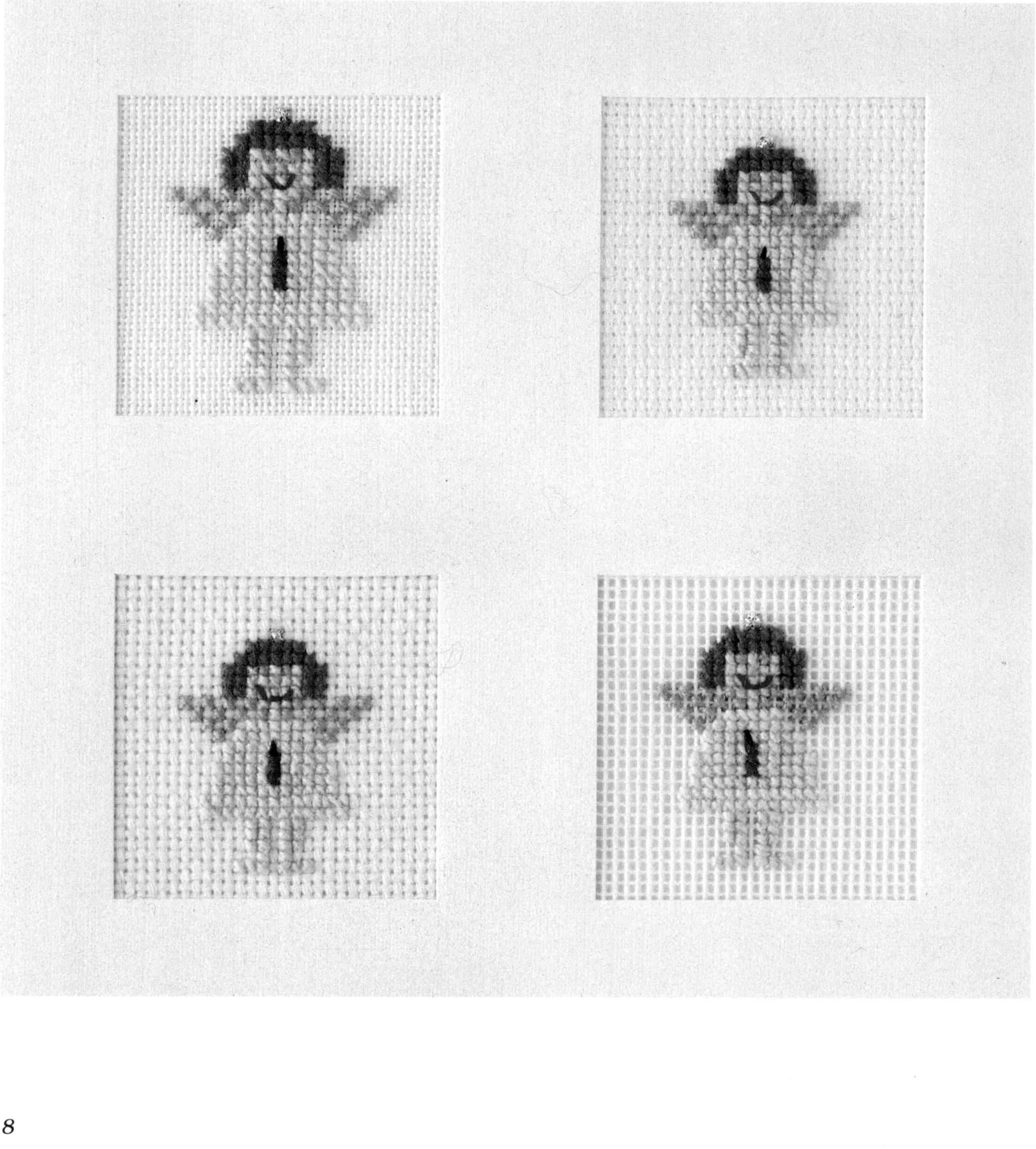

The samplers in this book were all made with MEZ embroidery floss; the charts show the MEZ numbers. For those who prefer DMC or J. & P. Coats embroidery floss, the following numbers are suggested as possible alternatives.

MEZ	DMC	J. & P. COATS
1	Snow-white	1001
2	ecru	1002
6	948	2331
8	754	2331
9	819	3280
10	3326	3126
11	892	3152
19	817	2335
22	304	3401
26	603	3001
29	600	3056
41	892	3152
42	498	3410
48	3689	3086
49	776	3086
50	963	3281
59	815	3000
68	326	3401
75	3354	3003
76	603	3001
77	309	3284
78	3350	3004
95	211	4303
98	550	4107
100	553	4097
107	550	4107
108	554	4104
109	553	4097
110	550	4107
112	208	4301
117	800	7021
120	828	7053
128	828	7053
129	800	7021
130	809	7021
131	799	7030
132	796	7100
133	824	7182
146	825	7181
158	828	7053
160	800	7021
161	793	7977
164	824	7182
167	3325	7972
185	747	7053
188	993	6185
300	744	2293
302	725	2298
303	972	2307
304	741	2314
305	783	2307
306	783	2307
308	921	3336
309	436	5943
316	920	3337
333	606	2334
335	891	3254
338	970	2327
341	918	3340
347	758	2337
351	355	2339
358	801	5475
359	300	5349
360	433	5471
363	436	5943
367	945	3335
369	919	2326
370	434	5000
371	433	5471
373	435	5371
374	434	5000
375	436	5943
378	435	5371
381	938	5477
382	898	5476
387	712	5387
390	739	5369
397	762	8510
398	415	8510
399	415	8510
400	414	8513
401	413	8514
403	310	8403
778	963	3280
832	433	5471
843	3012	6316
844	471	6010
846	938	5477
847	762	8510
848	415	8510
850	932	7050
851	823	7982
853	840	5379
854	640	5393
856	434	5000
860	3346	6258
862	367	6018
868	554	4104
869	211	4303
870	554	4104
871	3687	3088
872	902	3083
876	320	6017
878	701	6226
880	745	2296
884	920	3337
892	353	3006
893	776	3281
896	918	3340
897	3685	3089
901	783	2307
903	780	2298
905	838	5381
920	809	7021
921	809	7021
922	311	3336
926	739	5369
928	828	7053
939	809	7021
941	825	7181
943	782	2412
972	815	3000
975	747	7053

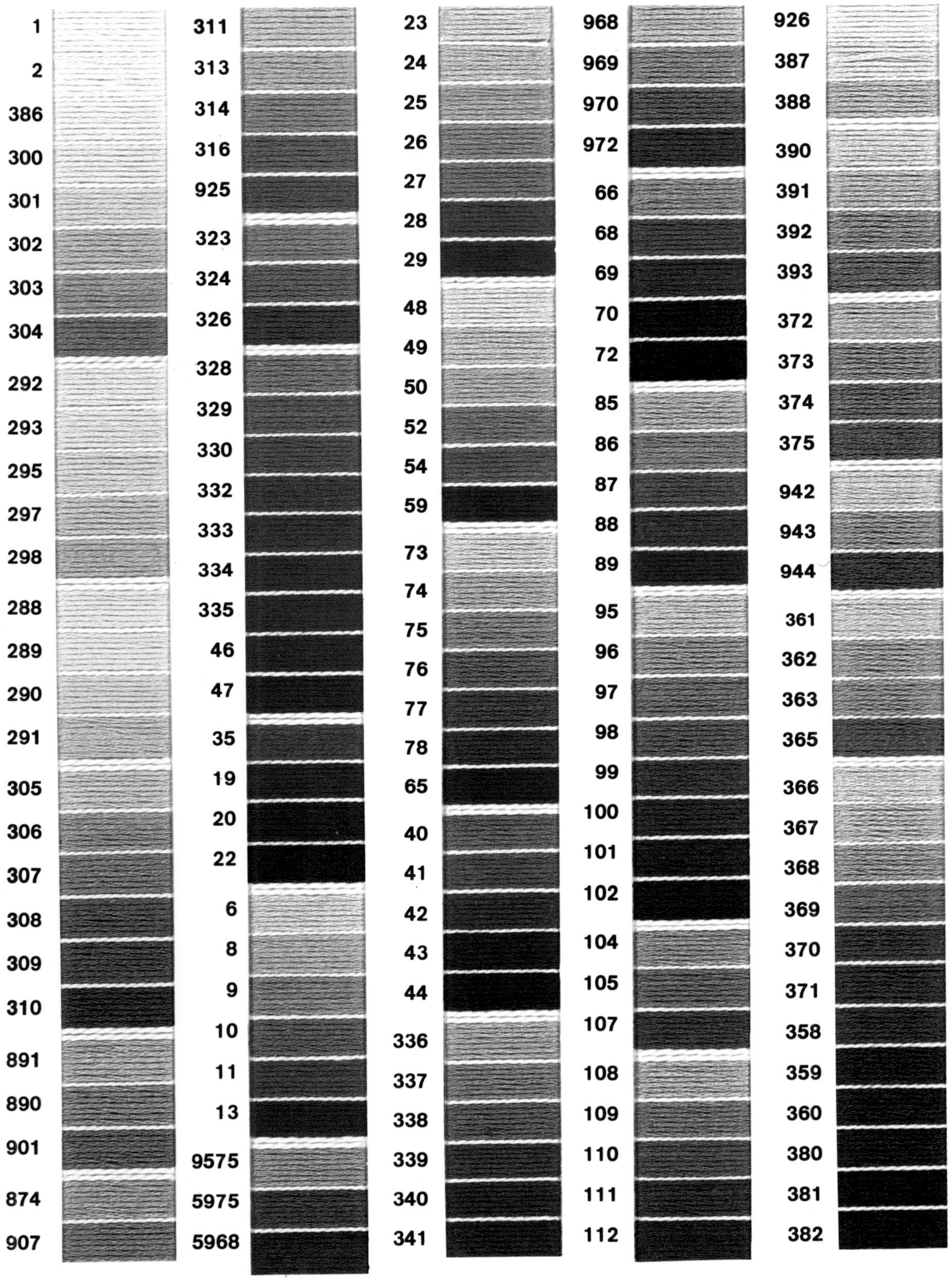

Color chart for MEZ embroidery floss

When buying the embroidery floss, please note the following: A zero in front of the color number of the wrapper around the floss means that the strand of floss is 8m (the normal length is 10).

347
349
351
352
355
357
933
376
378
379
936
956
945
278
279
280
281
924
264
265
266
267
268
269
259
260
261
262
263

253
254
255
256
257
258
238
239
240
241
242
243
244
245
246
225
226
227
228
229
923
203
204
205
230
213
214
215
216
217
218

206
208
209
210
211
212
185
186
187
188
189
167
168
169
170
928
929
930
433
410
158
159
160
161
162
164
975
976
977
978
979

117
118
119
939
940
941
120
121
123
127
128
129
130
131
132
133
134
144
145
146
147
148
149
150
152
397
398
399
400
401
403

885
886
887
888
906
830
831
832
898
889
903
905
852
853
854
856
842
843
844
845
846
858
859
860
861
862
875
876
877
878
879

900
8581
847
848
849
850
779
851
920
921
922
869
870
871
872
873
892
893
894
895
896
897
778
4146
868
914
880
881
882
883
884

246	168	13	970	112	840	372	905
54	185	46	266	244	75	397	900
298	403	133	288	40	398	146	373
324	2	279	65	100	188	926	903
109	117	77	8	85	123	47	48
96	118	381	382	291	242	400	35

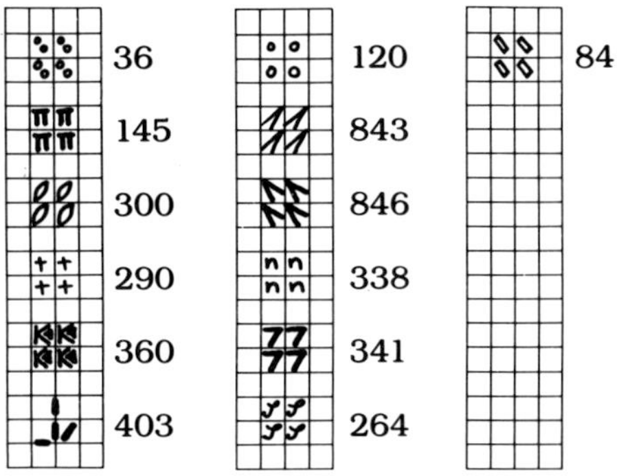
36
145
300
290
360
403
120
843
846
338
341
264
84

It is best to start this sampler in the middle of one of the packages and continue to work from there up, down, and sideways respectively.

Size of sample: 6¾ × 6 inches (17 × 15cm)

Time required: appr. 20 hours

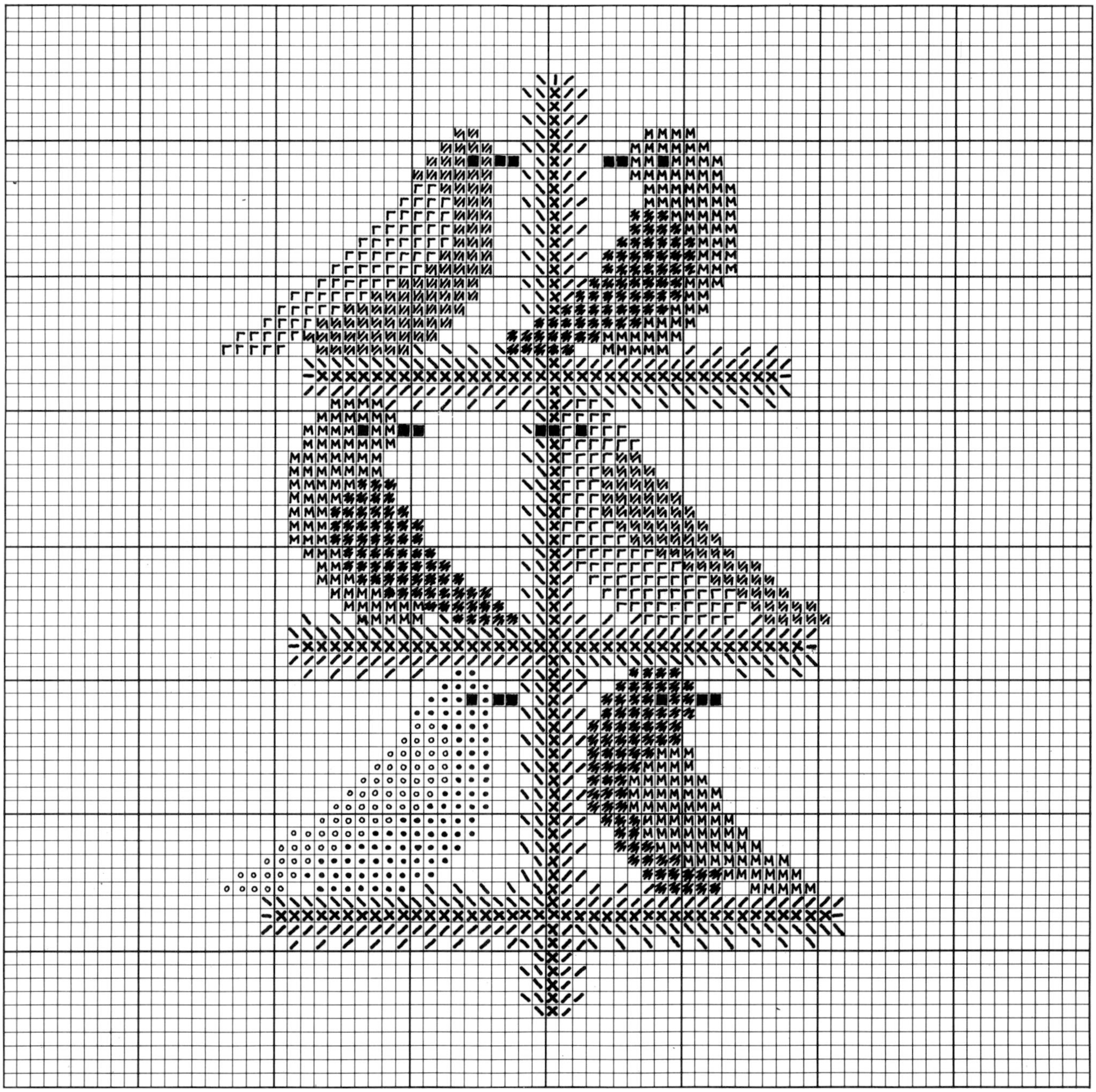

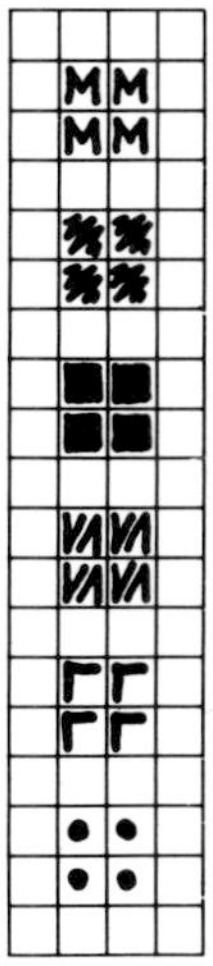

122

119

403

940

121

233

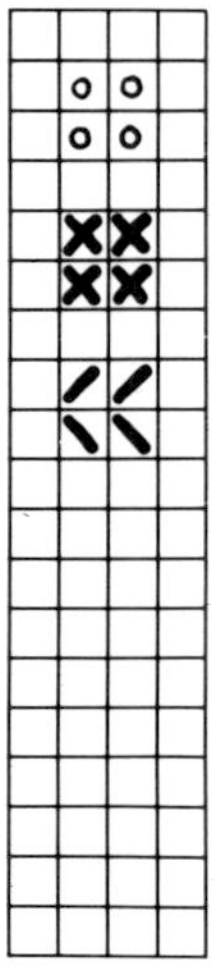

397

860

860
halfstitch

The colors and shapes of these feathered winter friends are reminiscent of Scandinavian embroidery.

The needles of the evergreen branches are half-stitches, alternating between under- and top-stitches.

Size: 4¾ × 3¼ inches (12 × 8cm)

Time: appr. 8 hours

These border motifs are particularly suitable for use in table runners, throws, and place mats. However, they can also be used individually to create greeting cards, napkin holders, or bookmarks.

The needles of the evergreen twigs are halfstitches pointing either left or right.

The pair of birds in the last row can be done as a separate motif (as shown in the left half of the row), or they can be done continuously (as shown in the right half).

The patterns for these motifs are on pages 18 through 21.

(#267: halfstitch; #403: wick; #268: halfstitch)

121
313
267
267 halfstitch
403 wick
301
47
324
46
59
398
73
146
403
268
268 halfstitch
269

906
393
298
119
48
117
372
145
35
397
2
49
118
358
269
891
400

890
360
920
849
847
218

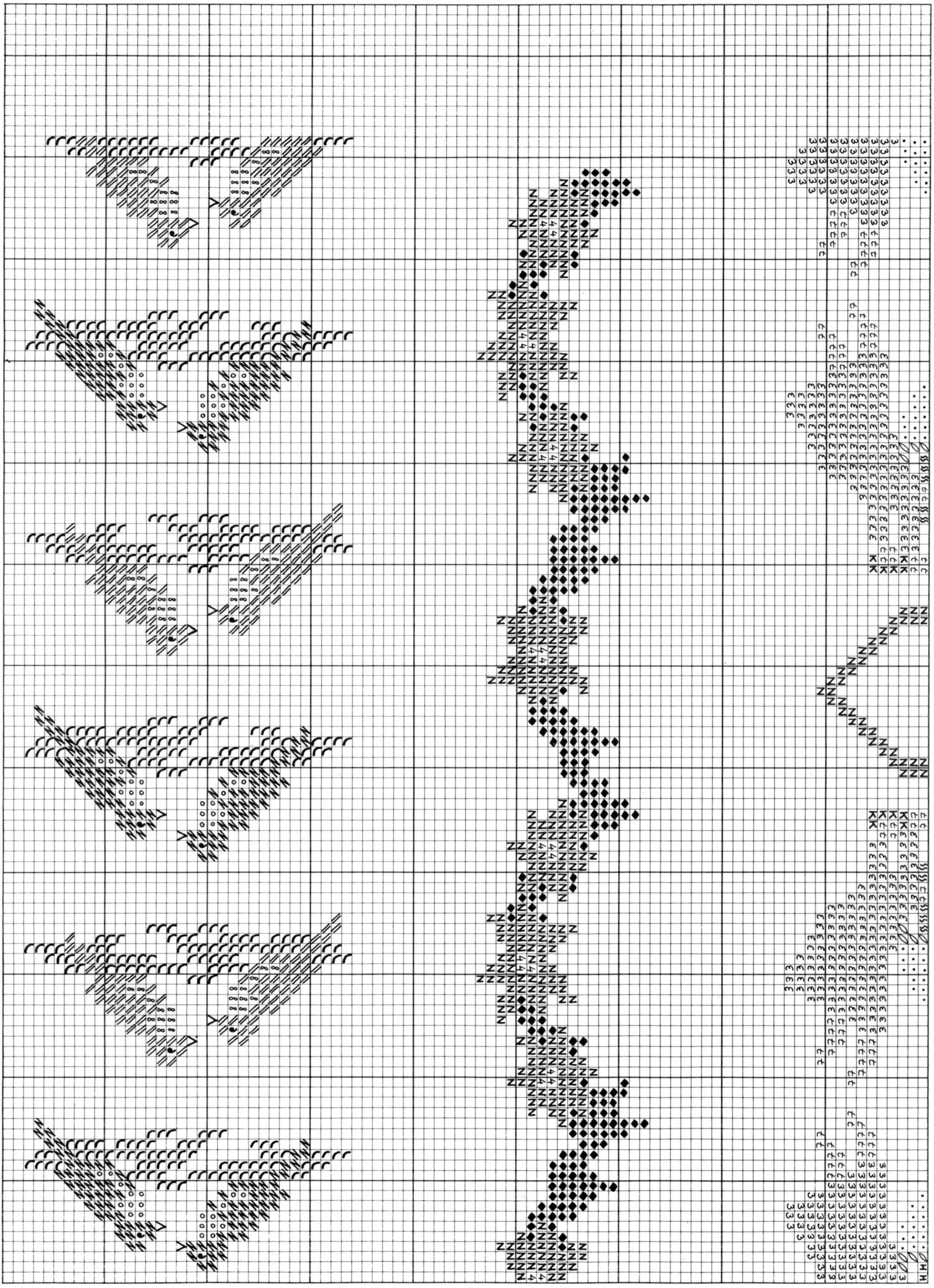

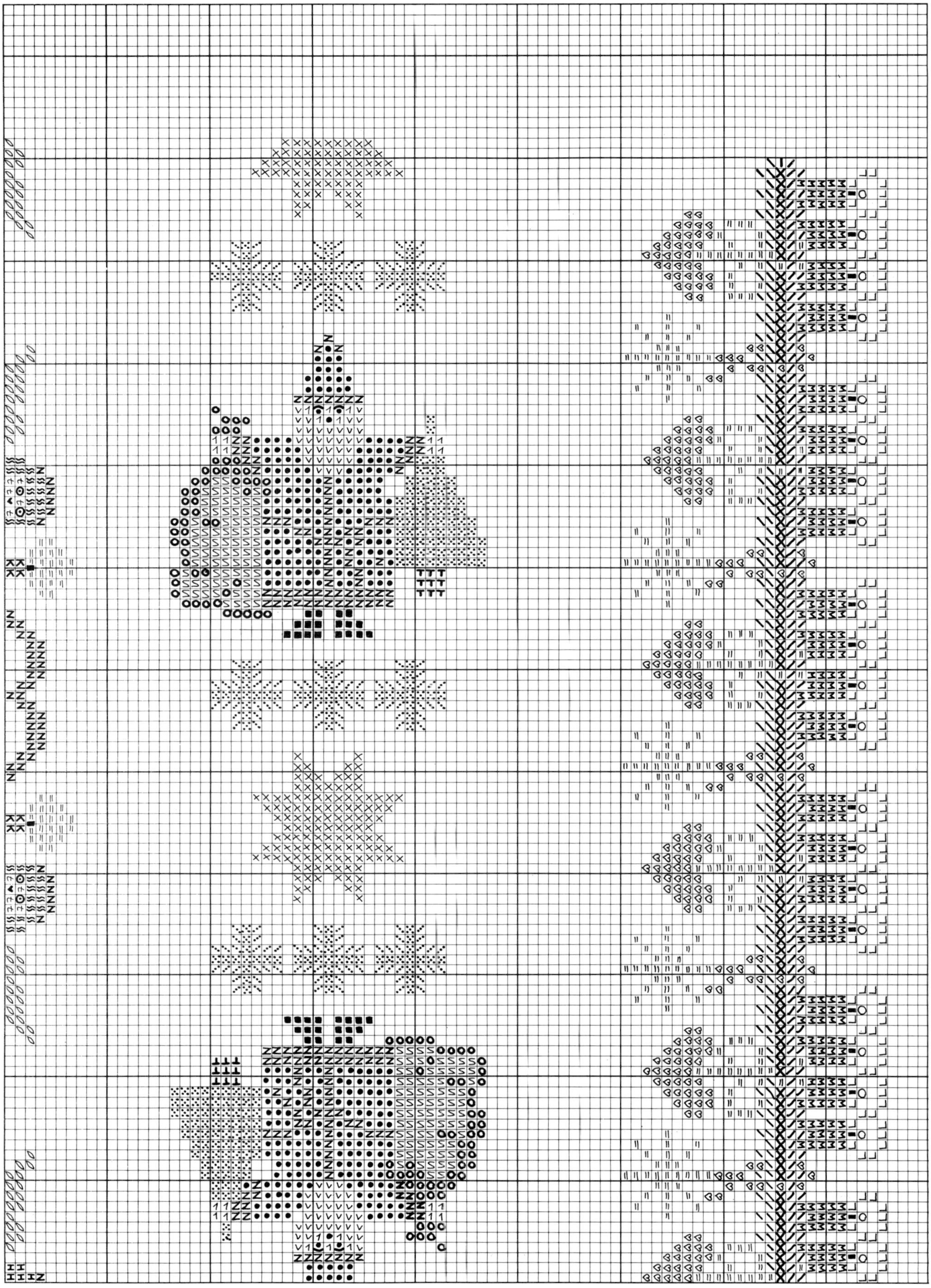

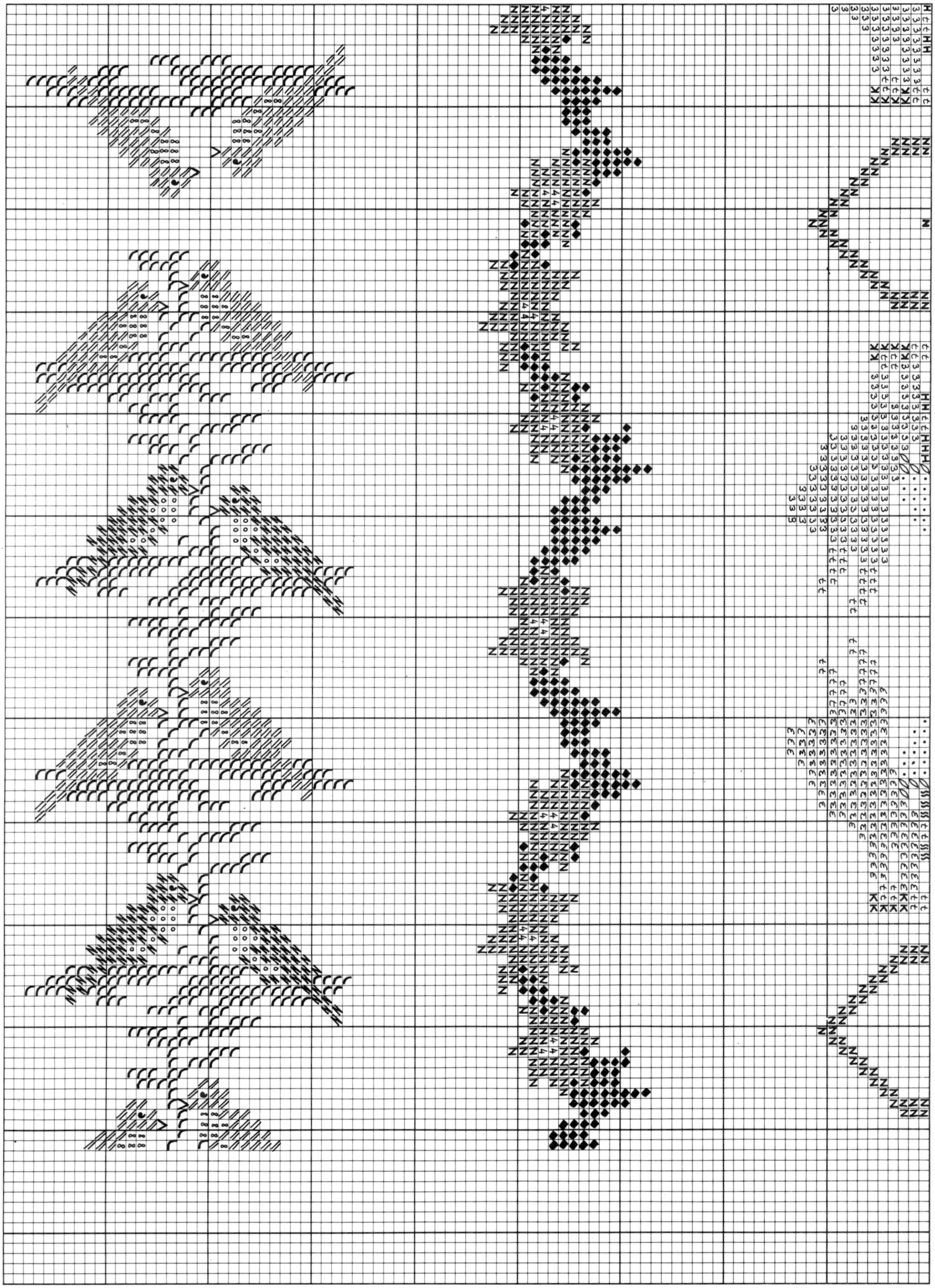

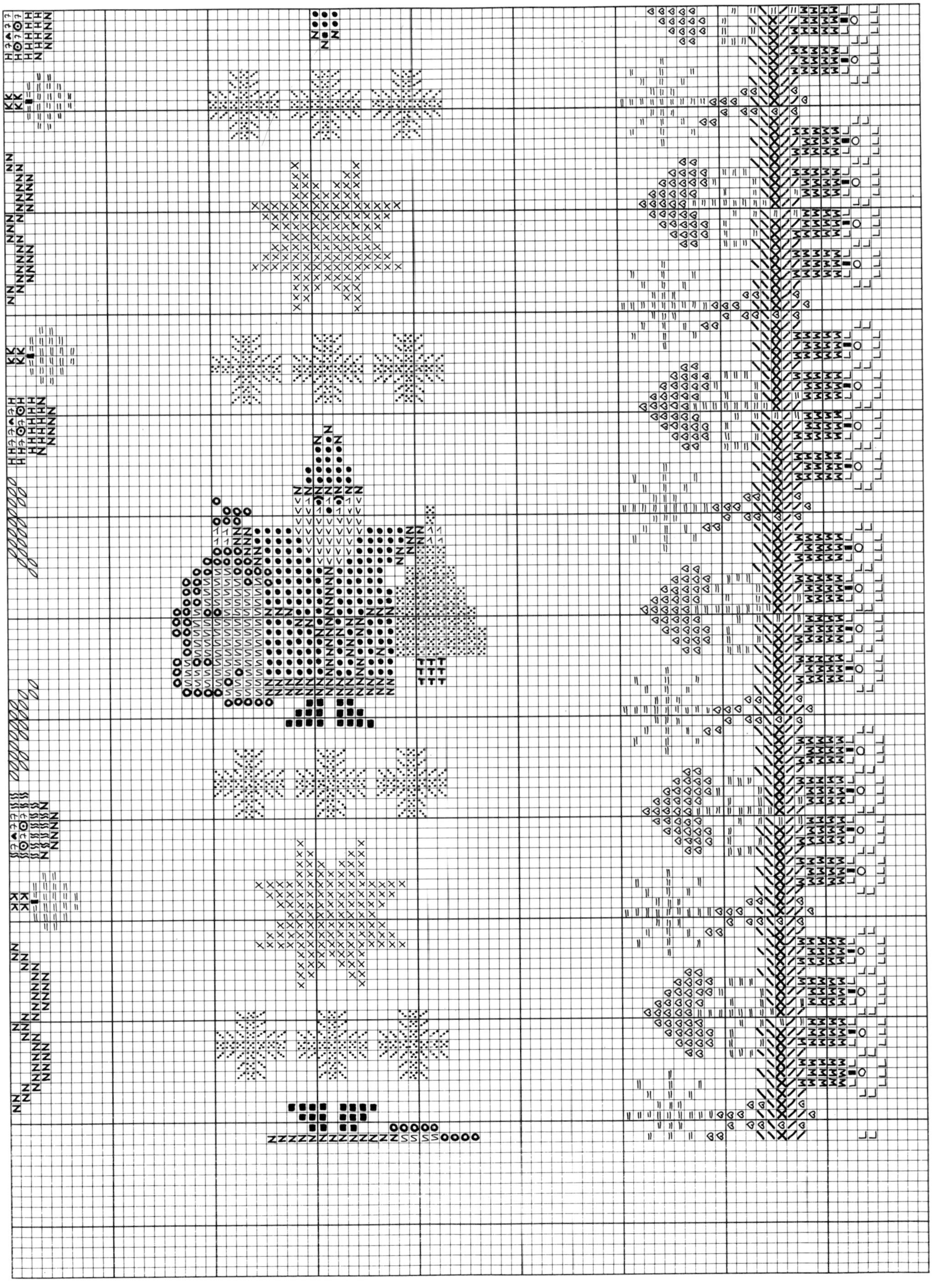

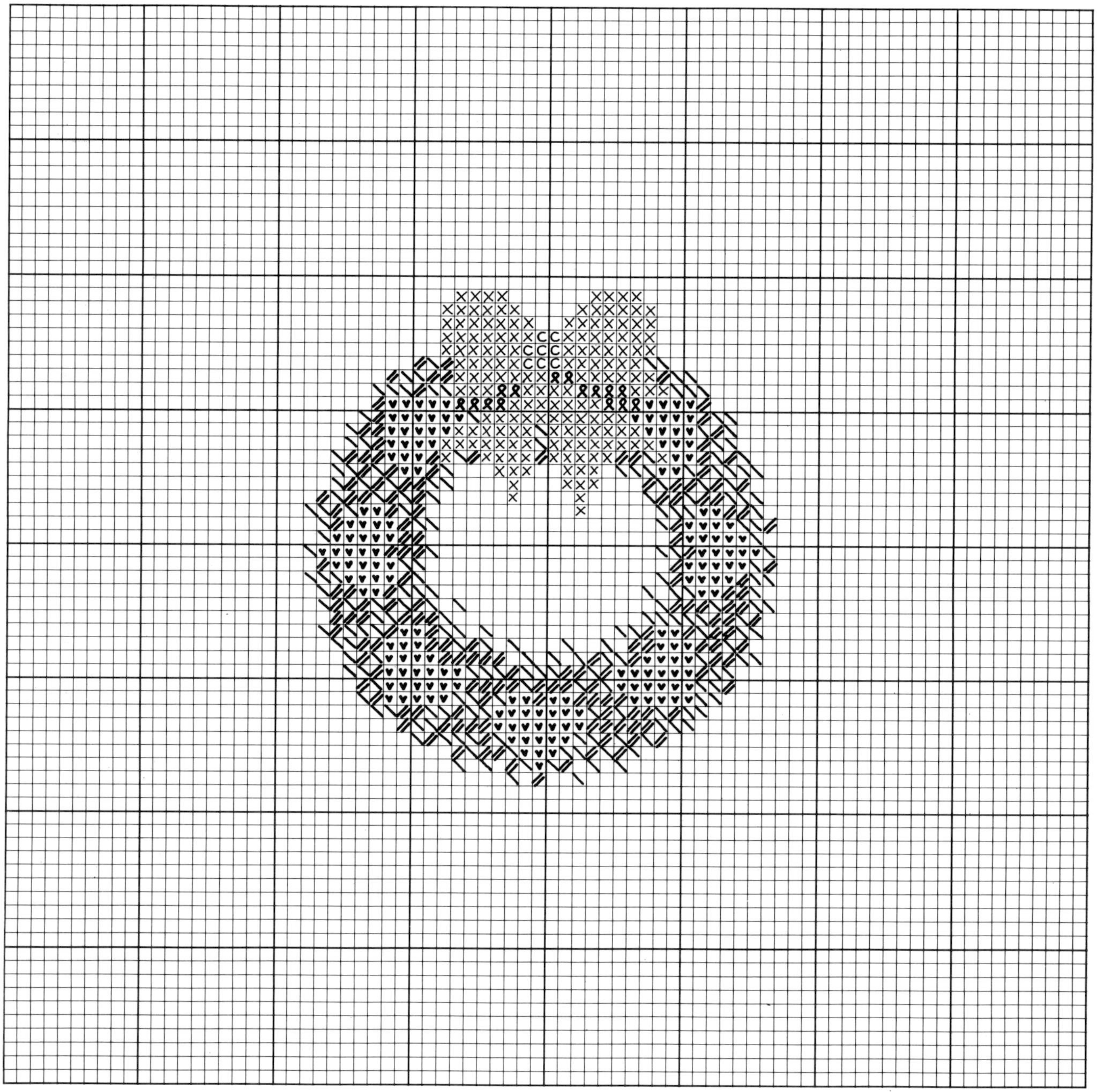

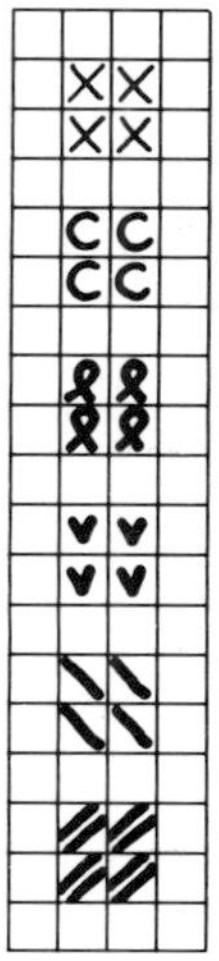

298

891

306

59

845

268

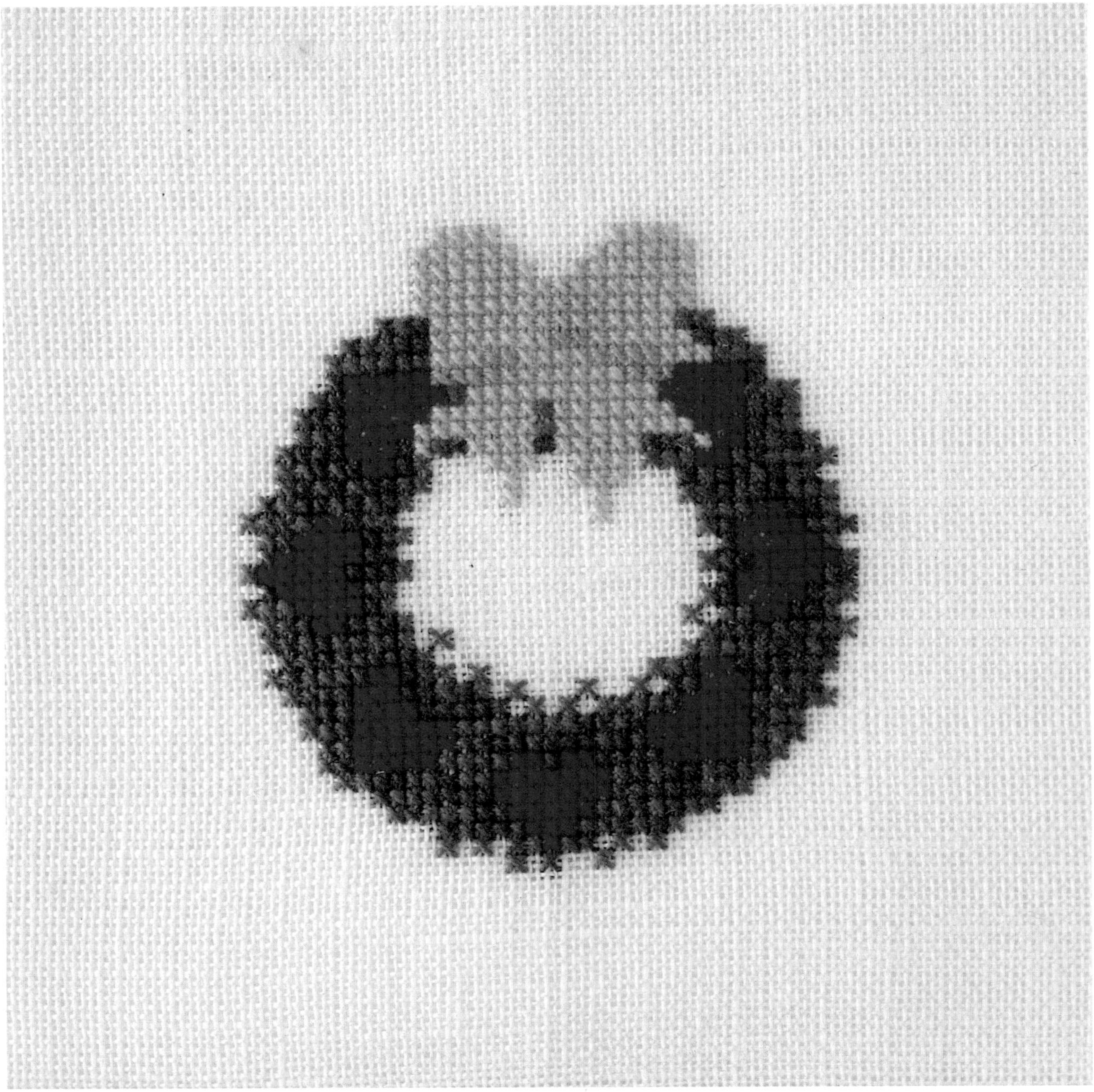

A pretty and easy motif—even for a beginner. It is best to start the project in the center of the bow, which acts as a point of orientation for counting the stitches that follow.

Size: 2⅓ × 2⅓ inches (6 × 6cm)

Time: appr. 5 hours

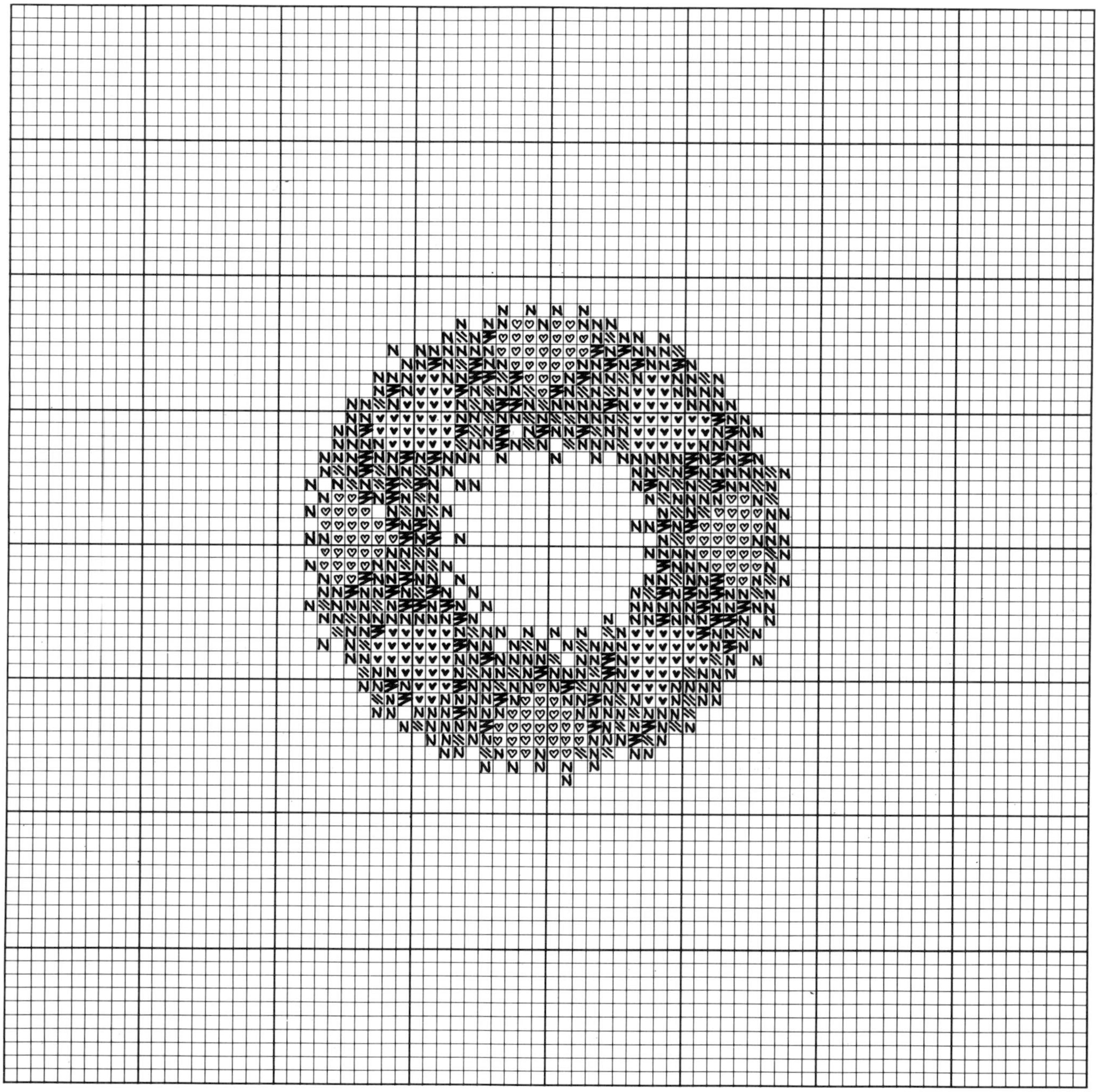

123

75

216

877

215

This wreath can be easily mastered by a beginner. Starting point should be the heart at the top of the wreath.

Size: 2¼ × 2¼ inches (5 × 5 cm)

Time appr. 5 hours

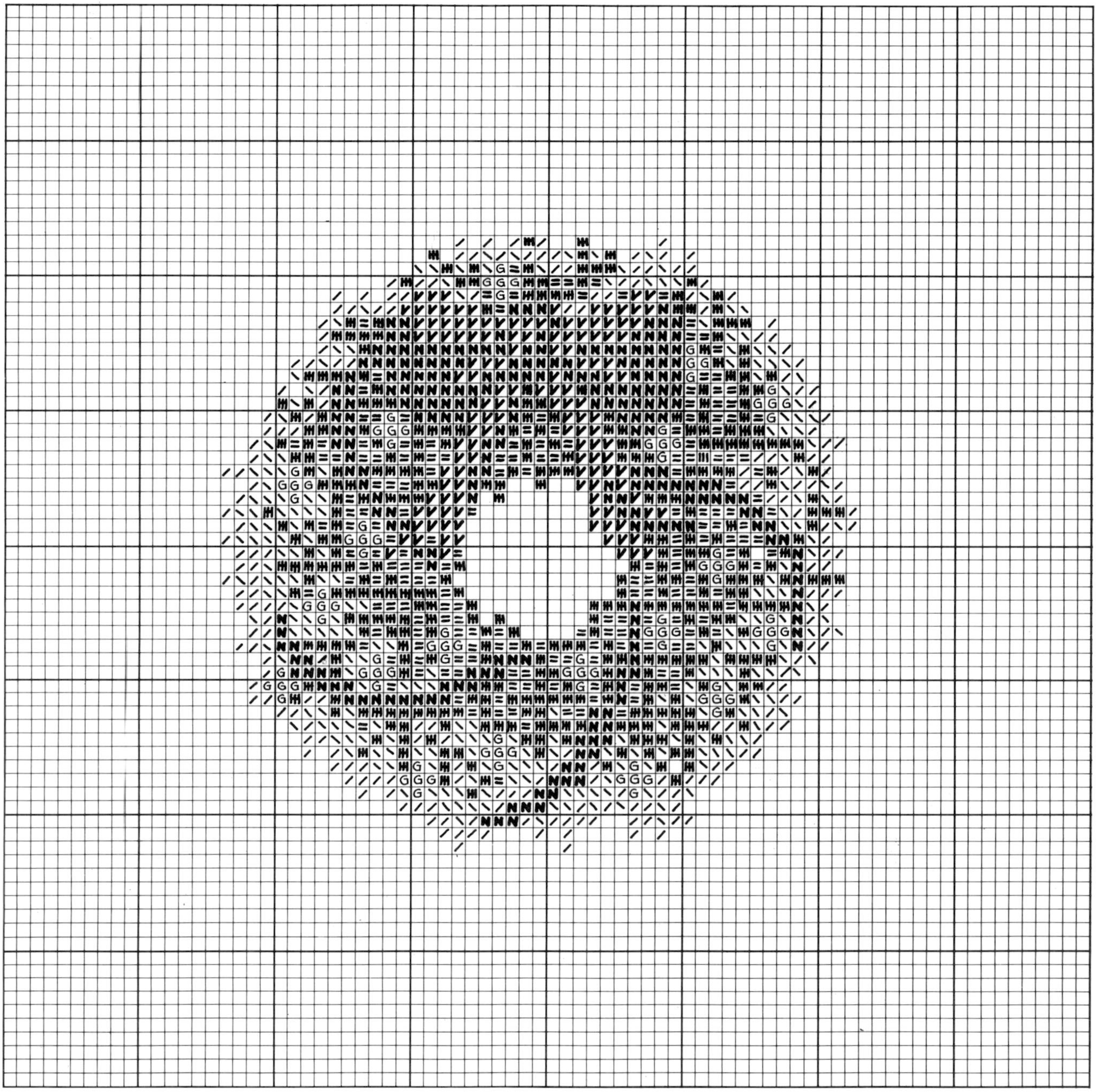

46	N	118
13	V	119
266	/	216
846	H	246
Gold	G	77
268	=	217
267	\	877

The sampler shown offers two different color combinations: one in the traditional red/green combination and the other in cool, Nordic colors. This provides examples of what can be achieved with different color schemes. Use your imagination and create your own.

Size: 3⅛ × 3⅛ inches (8 × 8cm)

Time: appr. 7 hours

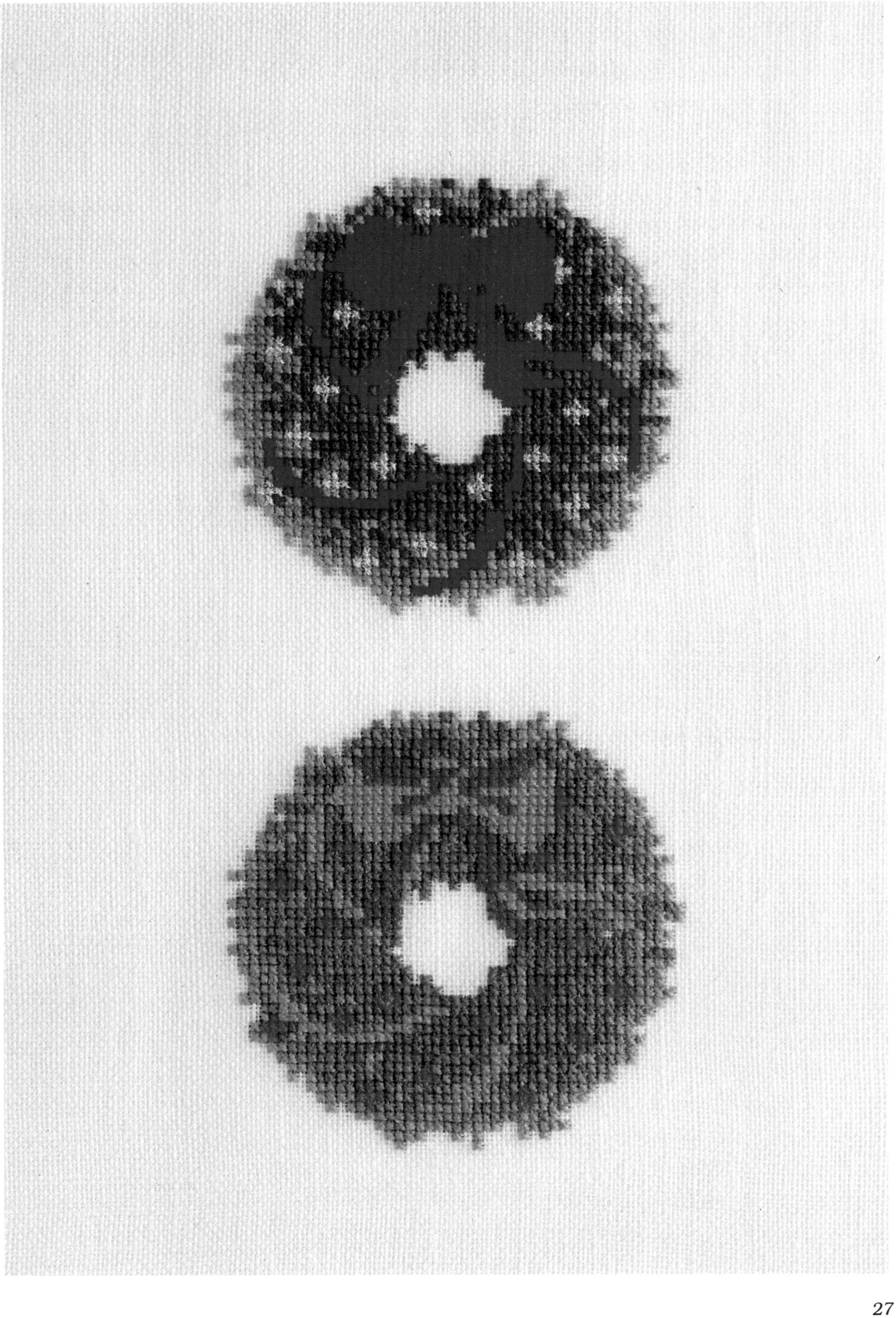

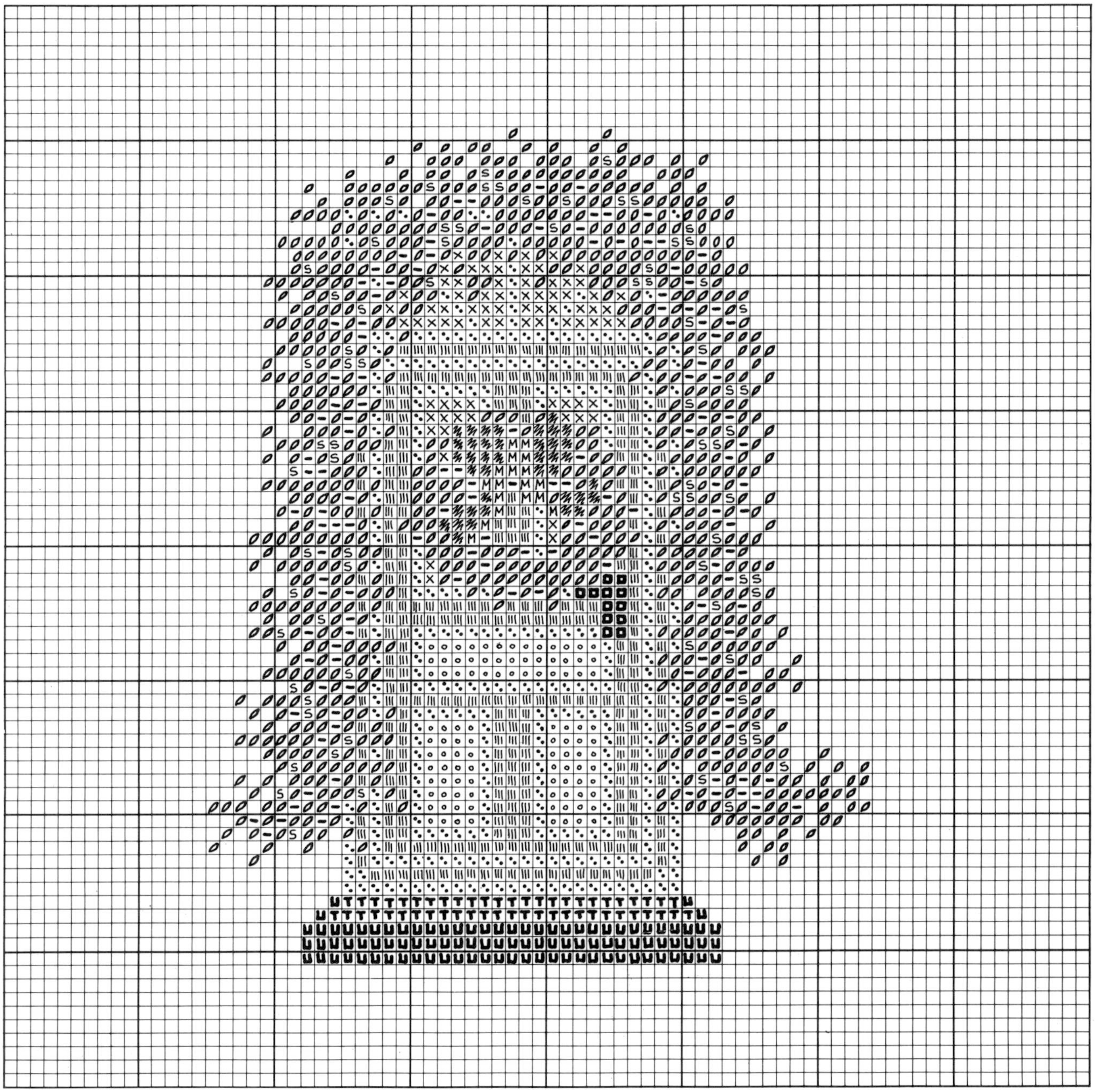

Symbol	Colour
Ø	268
S	Silver
–	846
∴	900
◘	400
X	298
|||	146
o	847
U	393
T	392
%	46
M	47

This door, decorated festively for Christmas, indicates the coziness that resides behind it.

Size: 4⅛ × 3⅓ inches (10.5 × 8.5cm)

Time: appr. 15 hours

(#381: halfstitch; S: silver)

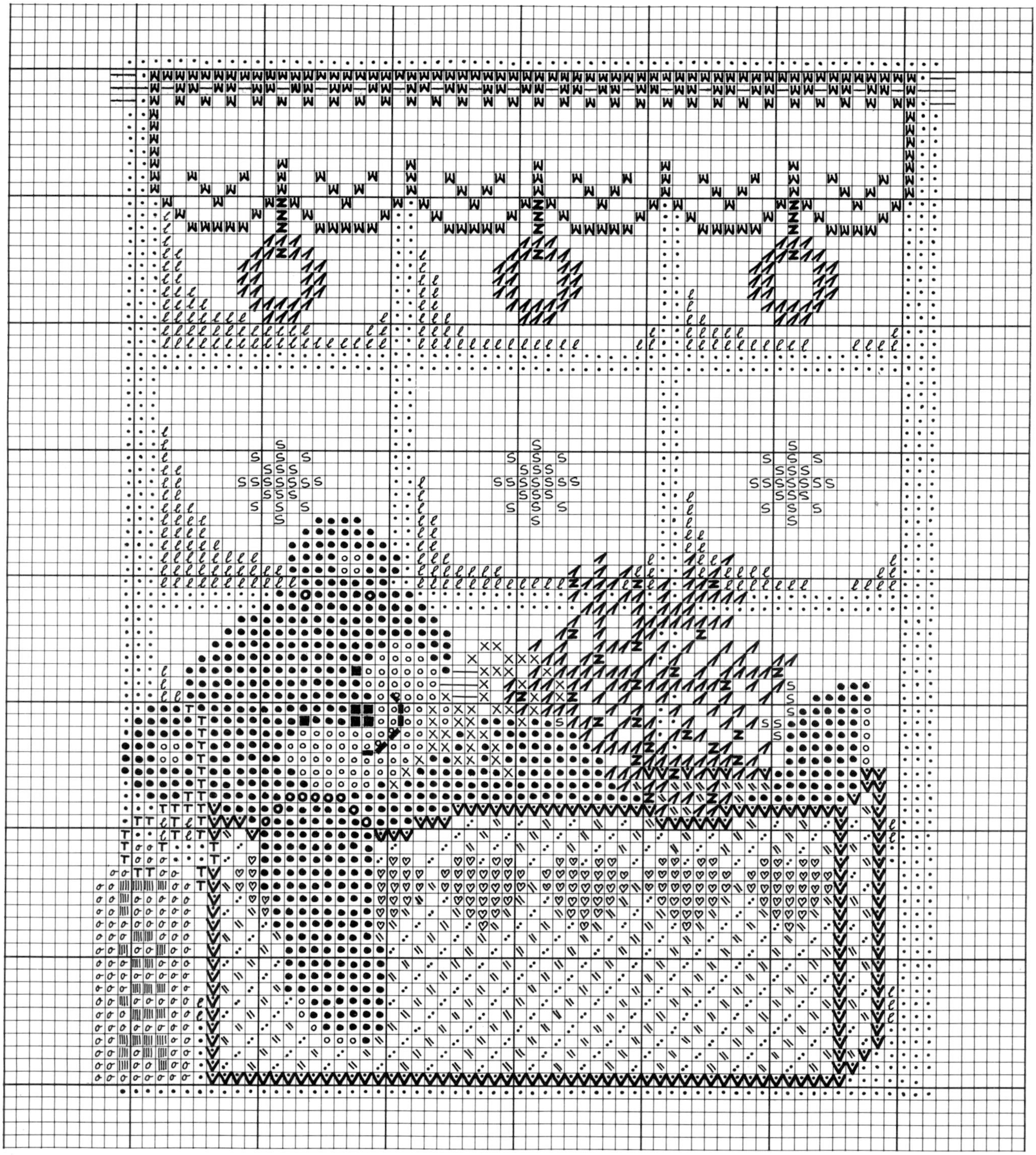

- 355
- 914
- 358
- 381
- 381 half
- 279
- 168
- 54
- 298
- 306
- 109
- 75
- 244
- 59
- 928
- 118
- 2
- 940
- 847
- Silver

This cheerful teddy bear, resting in a gift box, is undoubtedly looking forward to Christmas. Several hours should be set aside for this sampler by those who would like to enjoy the finished project.

Size: 5½ × 4⅓ inches (14 × 11cm)

Time: appr. 20 hours

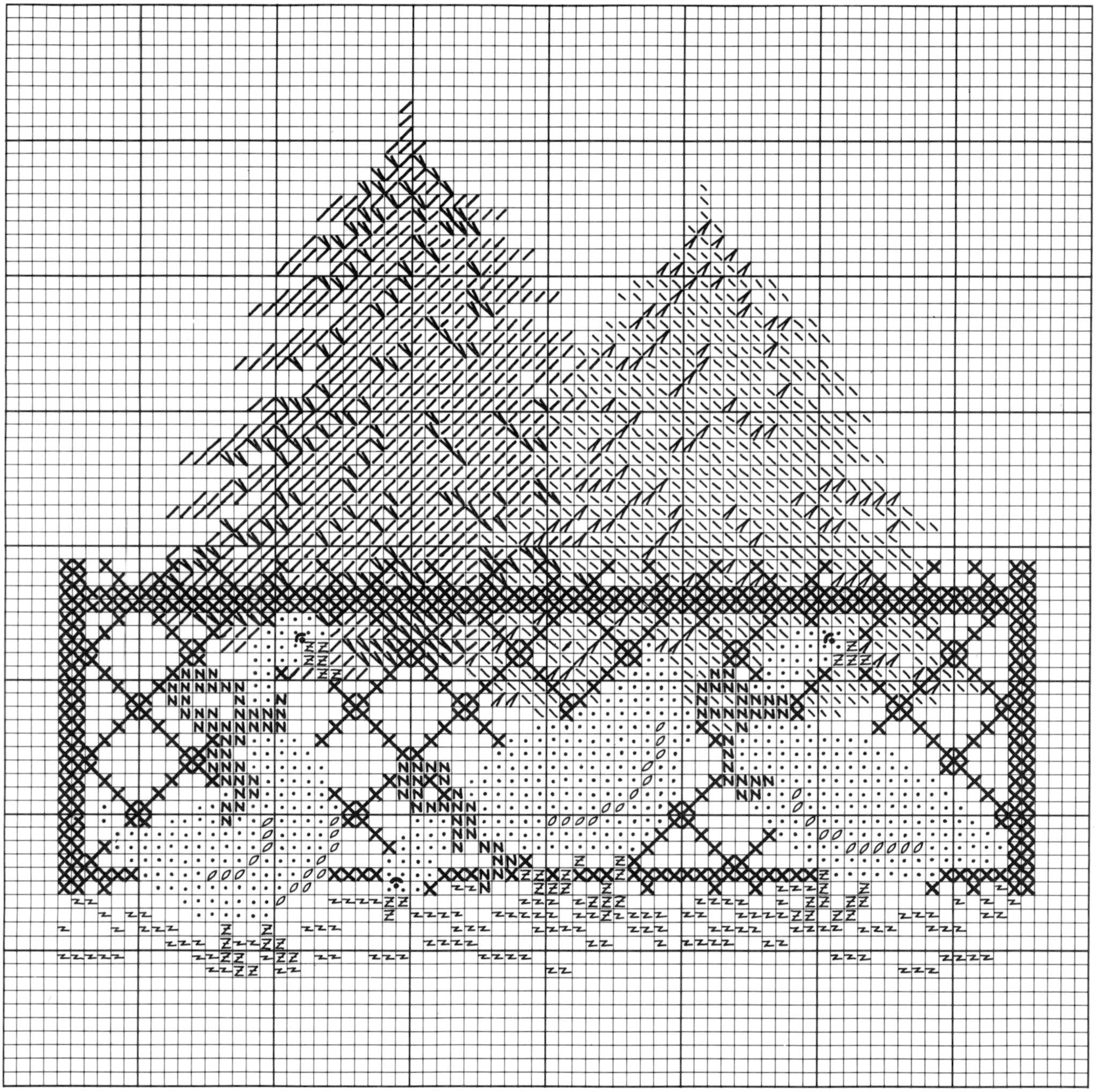

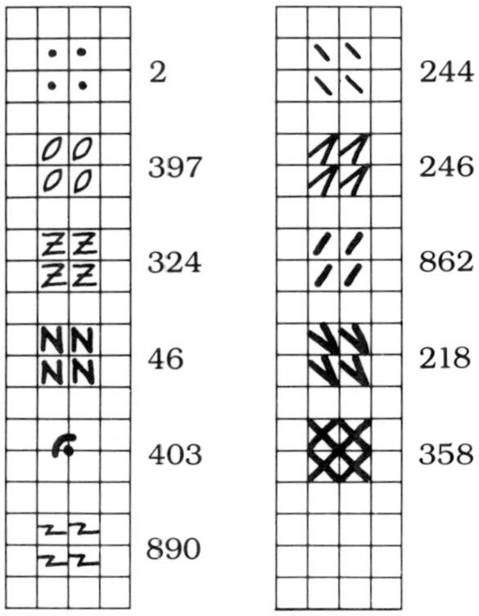
2
397
324
46
403
890
244
246
862
218
358

Instead of ending up in the oven for the Christmas dinner, these wonderfully decorated geese will survive and add to the festive decoration of many a holiday to come.

Size: 4¼ × 4¾ inches (11 × 12.2cm)

Time: 12 hours

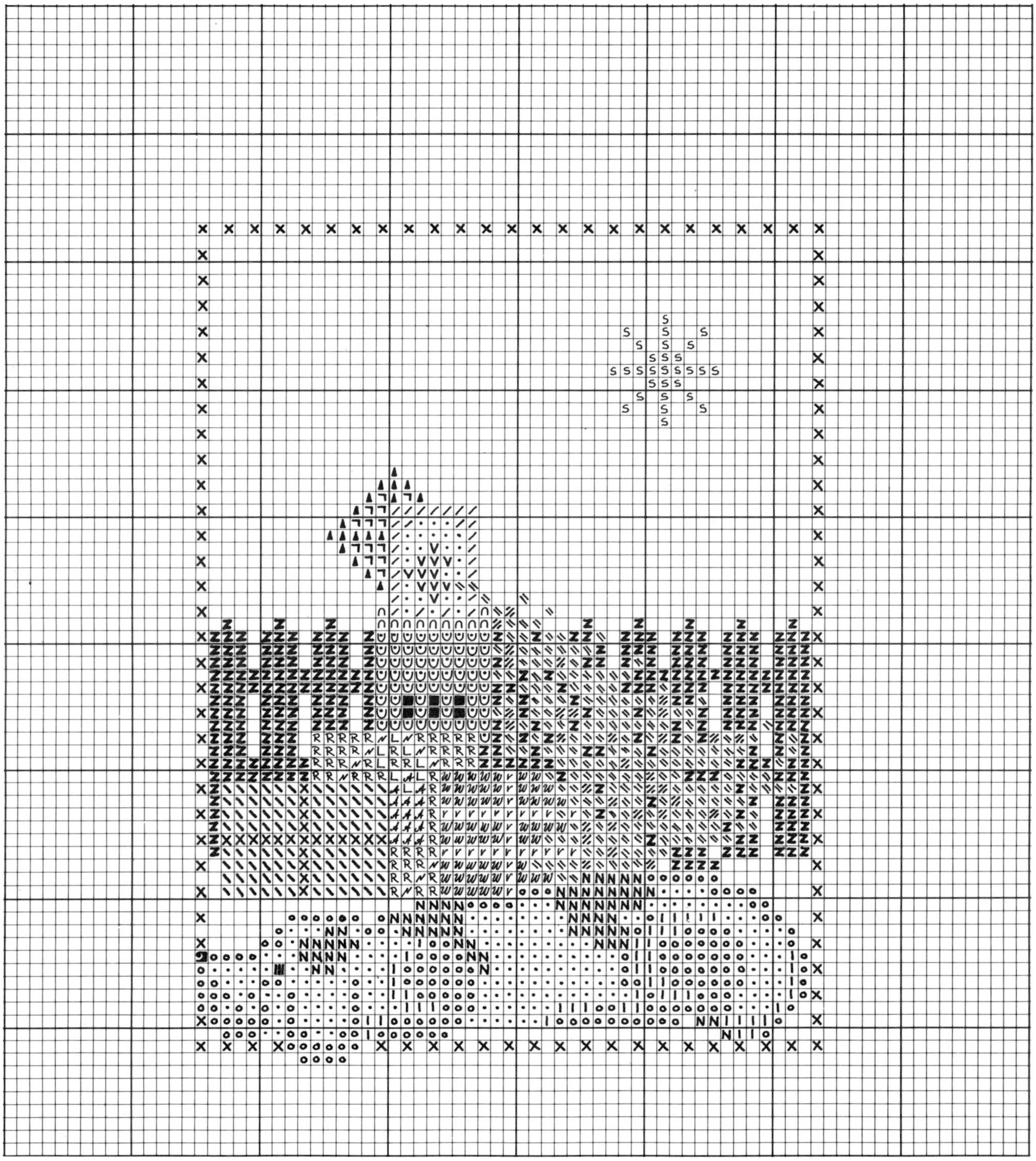

905	112	778	298	59	390	Silver
277	109	926	403	900	372	
268	121	75	88	399	907	
862	119	306	85	397	896	

The gifts that Santa has left at the garden fence are well guarded. Did he leave them there because he was afraid to come down the chimney? Those who love dogs should particularly enjoy this sampler.

Size: 4¼ × 3⅝ inches (11 × 8.5cm)

Time: 13 hours

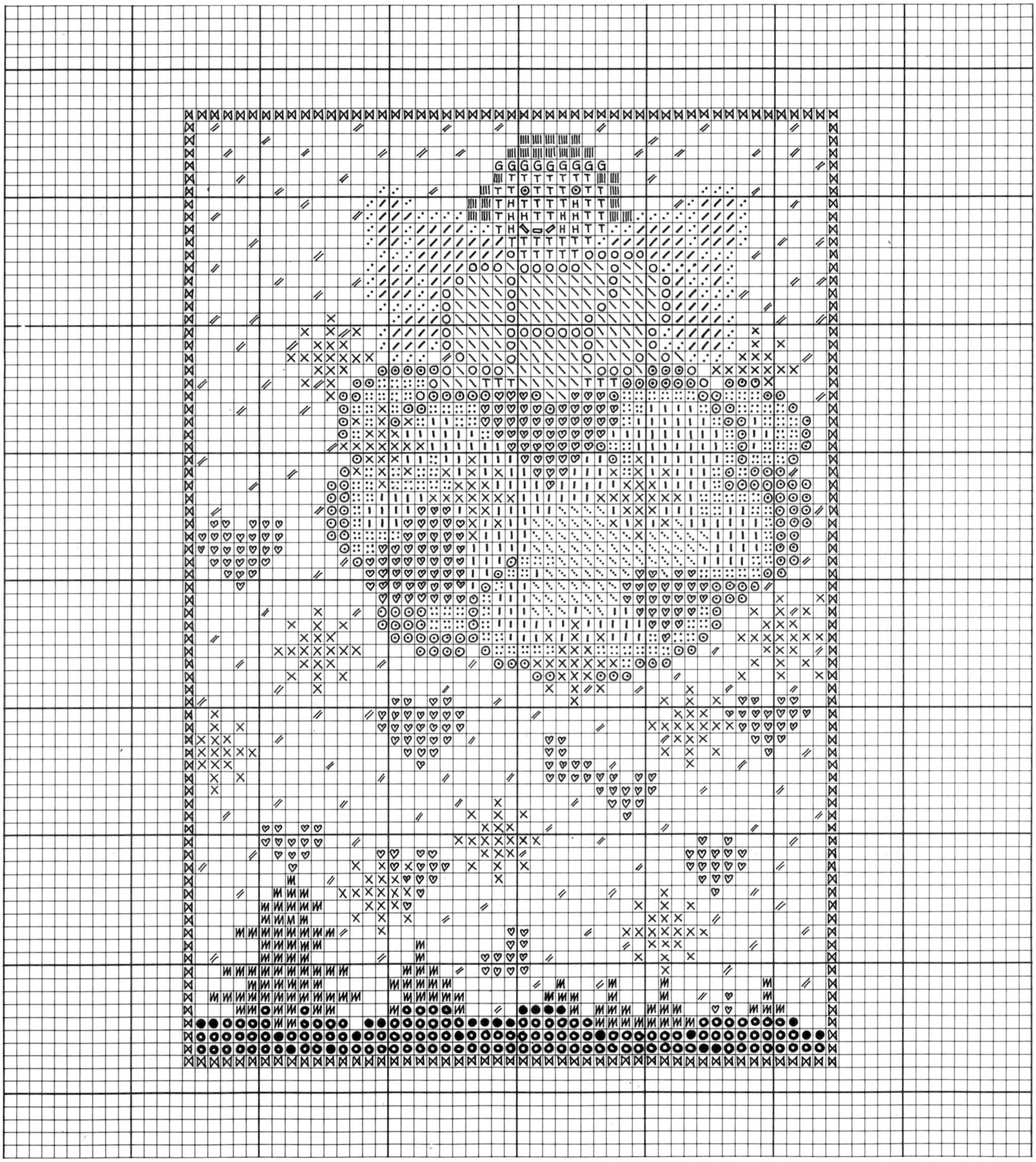

277	Gold	49	393	128
788	46 half	121	267	905
6	275	228	117	122
50	926	35	120	847

This sampler symbolizes Christmas. Perched on a cloud is an angel, hoping that the spirit of the season will reach everybody on Earth. There are stars that bring the message of Christmas, and hearts that represent love and warmth. This project is easy to complete.

Size: 5⅛ × 3½ inches (13 × 8.5cm)

Time: 8 hours

At last we know where Santa buys his clothes! Too bad we can't look beyond the display window.

This is a project for people with patience. The needles on the evergreen branches are half-stitches, either pointing to the left or to the right.

Pattern for this sampler is on pages 40 and 41.

Size: 6 × 8¼ inches (15.5 × 21cm)

Time: 38 hours

(Symbols #397: halfstitch; #905: straight-stitch; #19: straightstitch; #403: wick; G: Gold; #246: straightstitch; S: Silver)

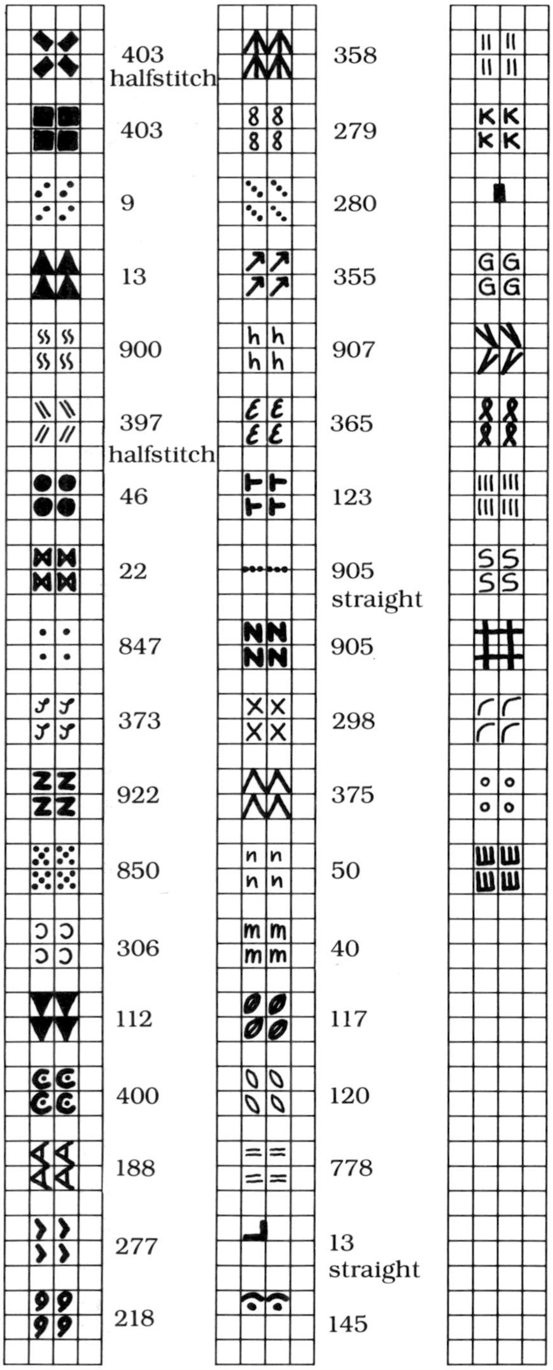

SHOP

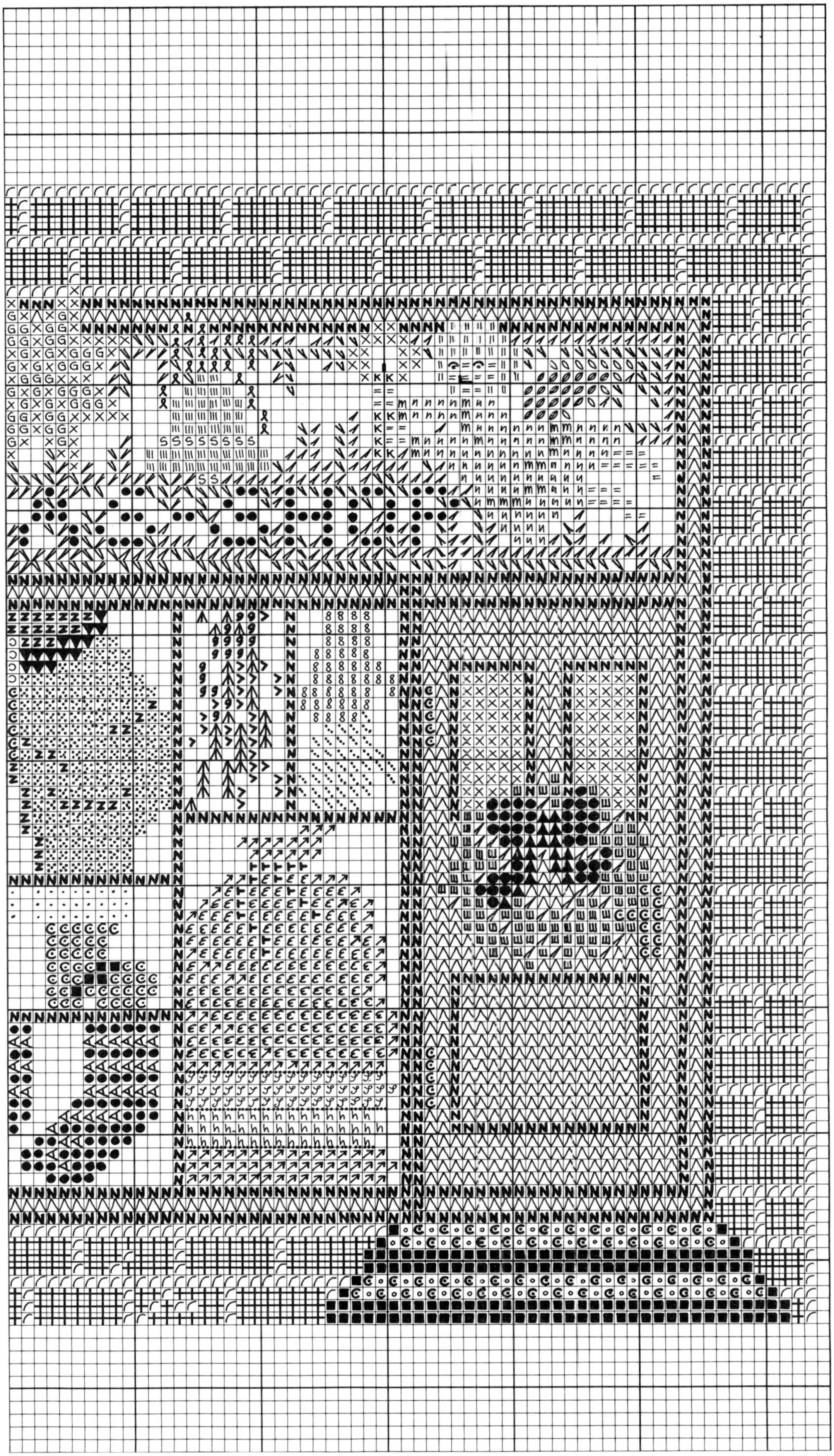

Relaxed and content, Santa Claus is on his way to his next stop, bringing gifts and the spirit of the season. Speaking of spirits, what do you think is in the bottle under his seat?

Size: 2⅝ × 7⅔ inches (6.6 × 19.5cm)

Time: 13 hours

(Symbols for #59: lips; #403: halfstitch)

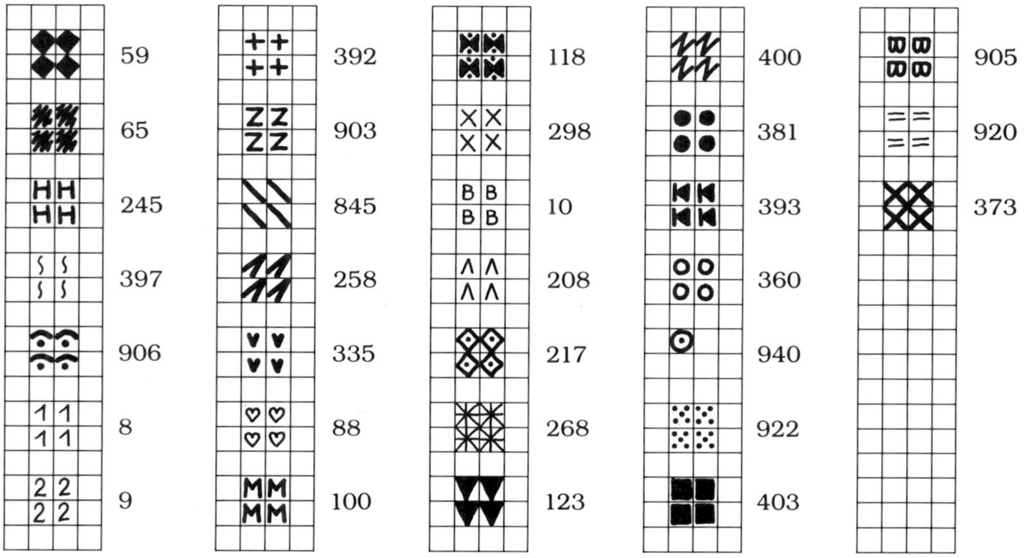
59
65
245
397
906
8
9
392
903
845
258
335
88
100
118
298
10
208
217
268
123
400
381
393
360
940
922
403
905
920
373

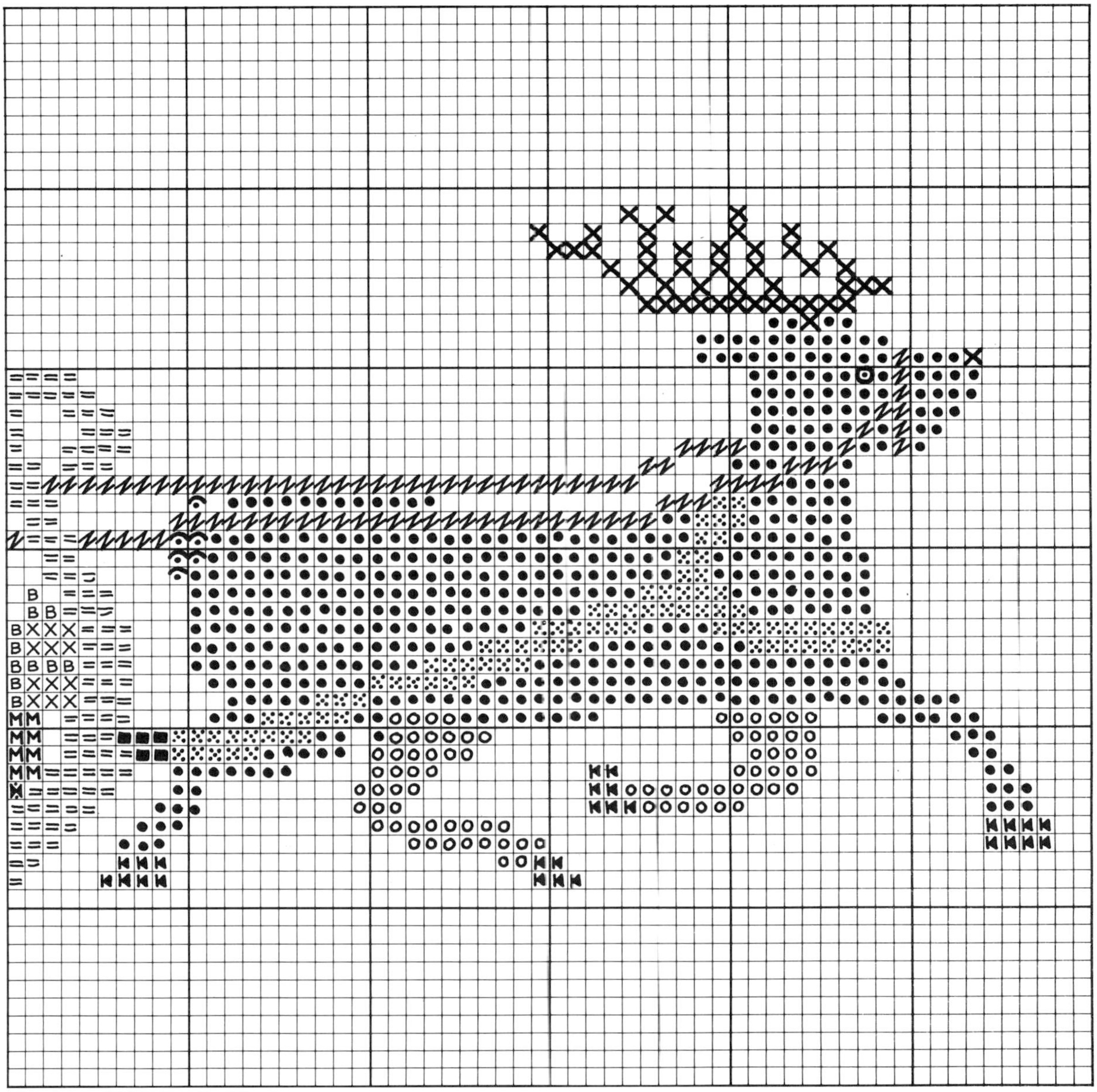

Zählmuster zum Schlitten-Motiv auf den Seiten 44 und 45

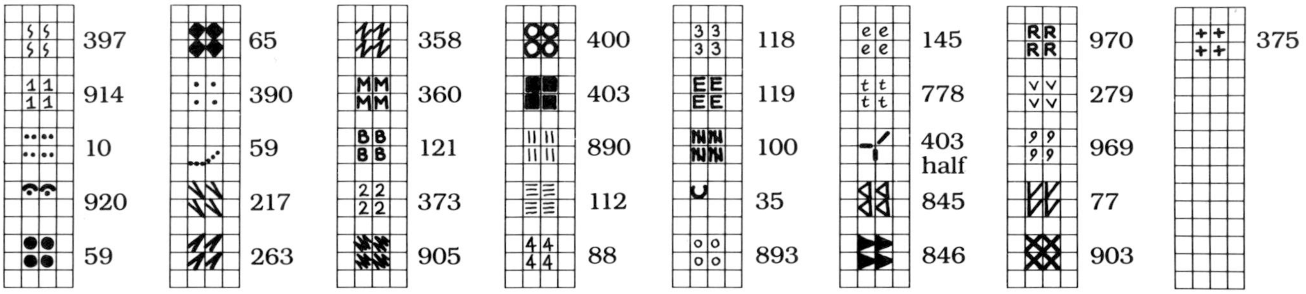
397
914
10
920
59
65
390
59
217
263
358
360
121
373
905
400
403
890
112
88
118
119
100
35
893
145
778
403 half
845
846
970
279
969
77
903
375

The inspiration for this Santa came from an old Christmas cookie mold.

Be careful when washing, since the dye in the red floss used for Santa's coat might bleed. When steam-ironing, put a protective layer of crepe paper between the finished sampler and the surface of the ironing board so that the excess dye can be absorbed into the protective material. Embroidery is always ironed face down. If a damp cloth is used instead of the steam-ironing method, make sure that it is almost dry.

Size: $7\frac{1}{4} \times 6\frac{1}{4}$ inches (18.5×15.5cm)
Time: appr. 18 hours
(Symbol #46: lips)

Symbol	No.	Symbol	No.	Symbol	No.	Symbol	No.	Symbol	No.	Symbol	No.	Symbol	No.
T	893	N	246	i	392	ʌʌ	920	//	847	ᘐ	843	‡	373
t	778	⫽	244	Z	846	ᒋ	849	z	328	VA	845	=	390
⁖	9	■	403	⋋	269	8	381	B	326	7	900		
◈	46	O	897	G	Gold	‖‖	262	∞	905	L	400		
⌒	146	$	372	2	290	V	392	‹	339	K	47		
⊙	969	ℱ	22	H	355	3	88	⁙	280	▪	403 wick		
8	903	●	896	∩	365	\	306	U	123	2	290		
X	298	↗	393	h	907	1	890	/	121	∘	128		

On a crisp, starry night, three children singing Christmas carols bring us the joyous news of Christ's birth. What could be more traditional? Note that the lips of the children are a combination of vertical and horizontal, straight half-stitches. The eyes can be done in either cross-stitch or in small knot-stitches.

Size: 7 × 6 inches (17.5 × 15cm)

Time: 18 hours

(Symbol #683: halfstitch; #246: halfstitch)

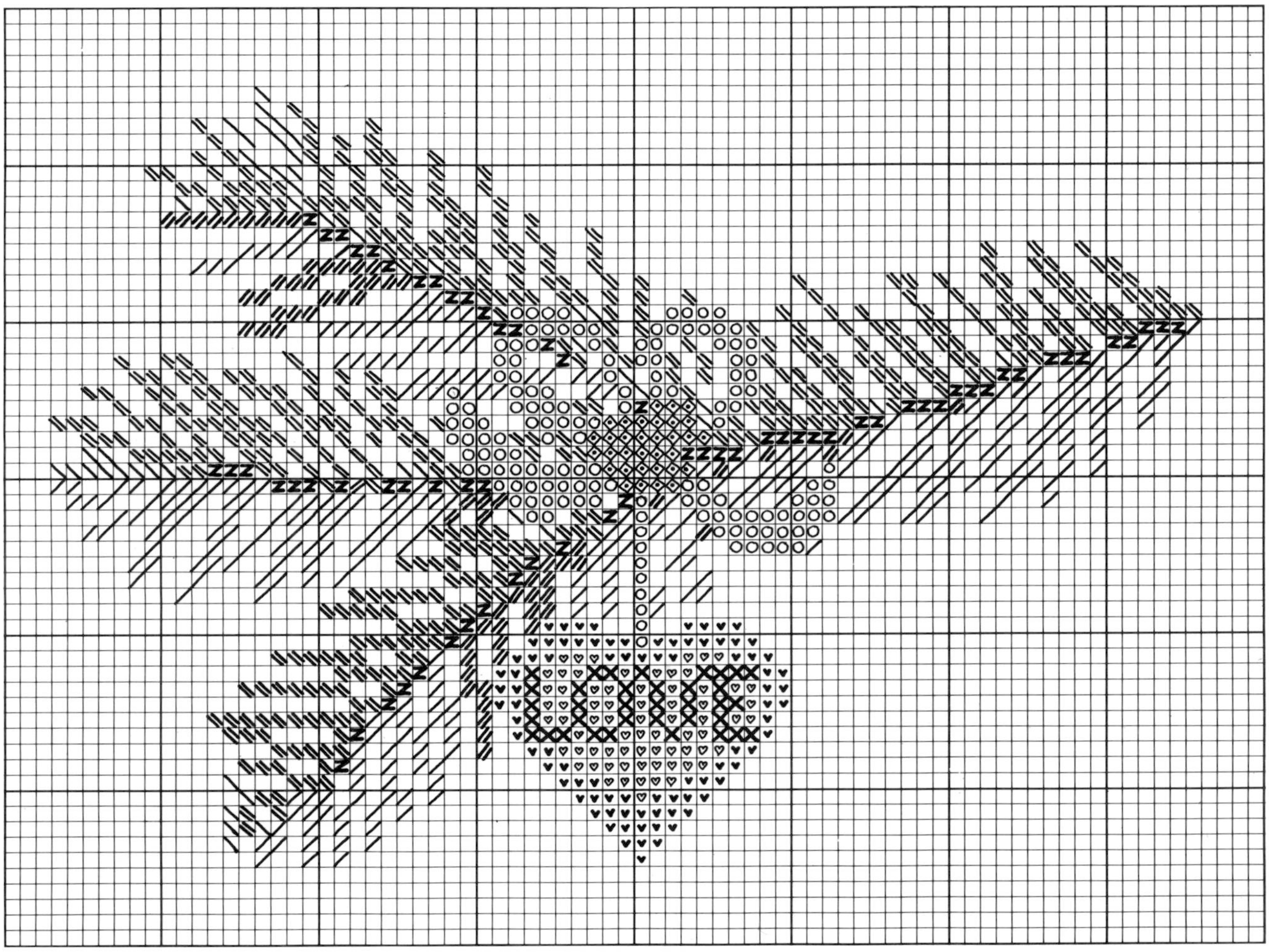

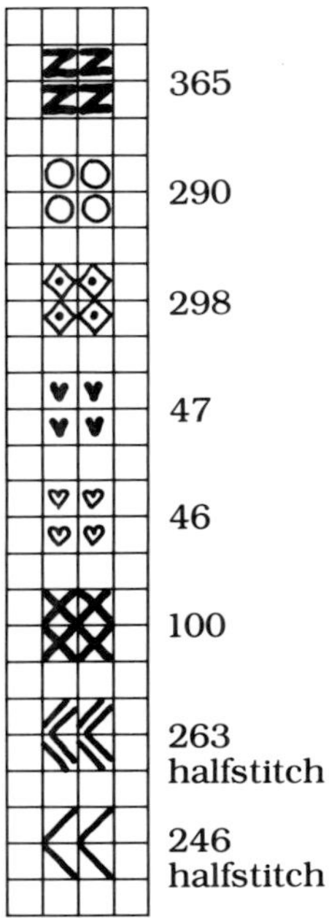
365
290
298
47
46
100
263 halfstitch
246 halfstitch

This sampler requires close attention. It is easy to lose count when working the halfstitches of the evergreen branches. It is best to start in the center with the yellow bow, then do the heart, and work from there to the outside.

Size: 4 × 5⅛ inches (10 × 13cm)

Time: 6 hours

Above: The sampler for the pattern on the opposite page.

Below: Symbols for the sampler on page 52.

146	88	65	123	290	232	244	847
398	112	35	218	306	778	358	326
905	862	Silver	59	890	920	188	313
846	46	Gold	400	393	128	118	860
267	98	121	403 wick	401	49	109	

Symbols for this pattern are on page 51.

Santa was here!

The lips of each of the angels are done in one straight, vertical stitch, and one halfstitch. The eyes are small knot-stitches. The wreath on the door is made with one vertical stitch each in silverfloss between two green cross-stitches. While the door panel is made with full cross-stitches, the frames around them are halfstitches, running alternately in opposite directions.

Time appr. 20 hours

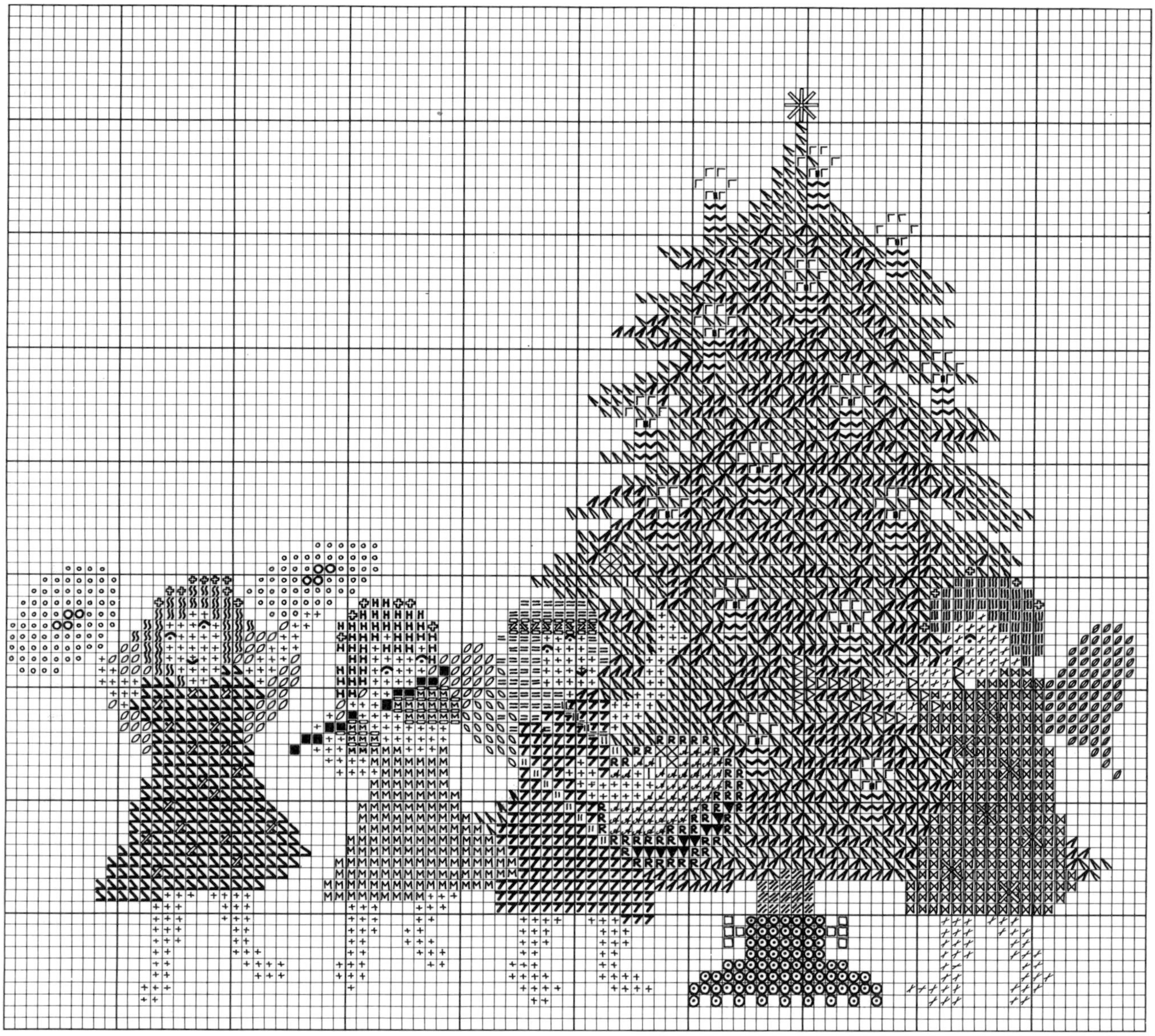

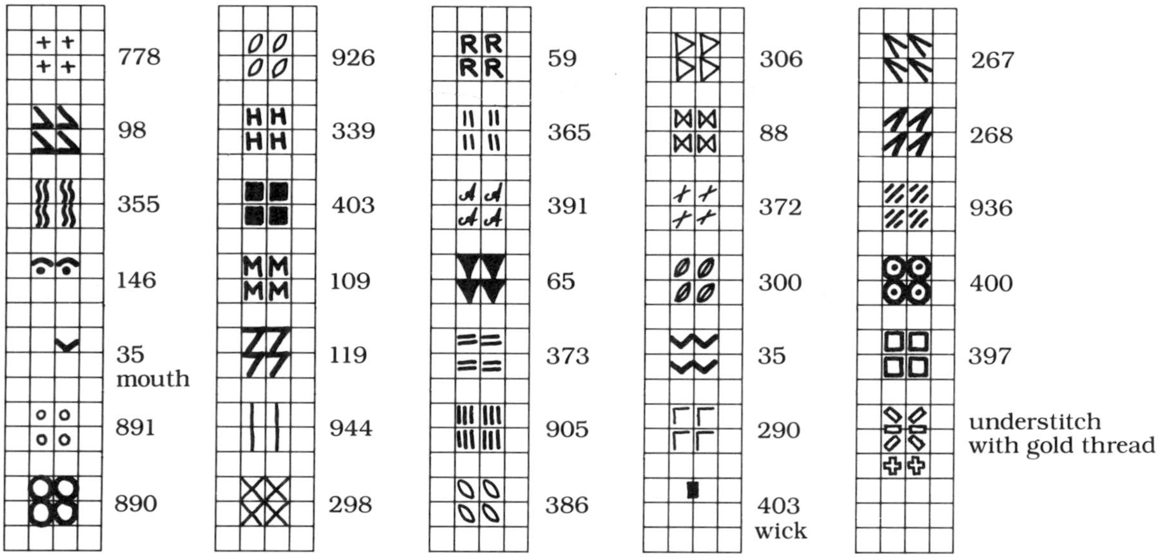

778
98
355
146
35
mouth
891
890
926
339
403
109
119
944
298
59
365
391
65
373
905
386
306
88
372
300
35
290
403
wick
267
268
936
400
397
understitch
with gold thread

The inspiration for this sampler came from a Christmas carol of the year 1623, which speaks of angels singing, playing the recorder, the drums, and the cymbals: all rejoicing in the spirit of the season.

Size: 5½ × 6¾ inches (13.5 × 17cm)

Time: appr. 13 hours

This sampler extends wishes for a Merry Christmas in ten languages. (Color design: Angela Kerzel.) Of course each individual motif can be used separately in combination with the language appropriate to the person for whom it is intended. Choice of colors can be changed also. This might be an ideal project for using leftover floss. Pattern for the sampler is on pages 58 and 59.

Size: 12 × 9¼ inches (30 × 23.5cm)
Time: 50 hours

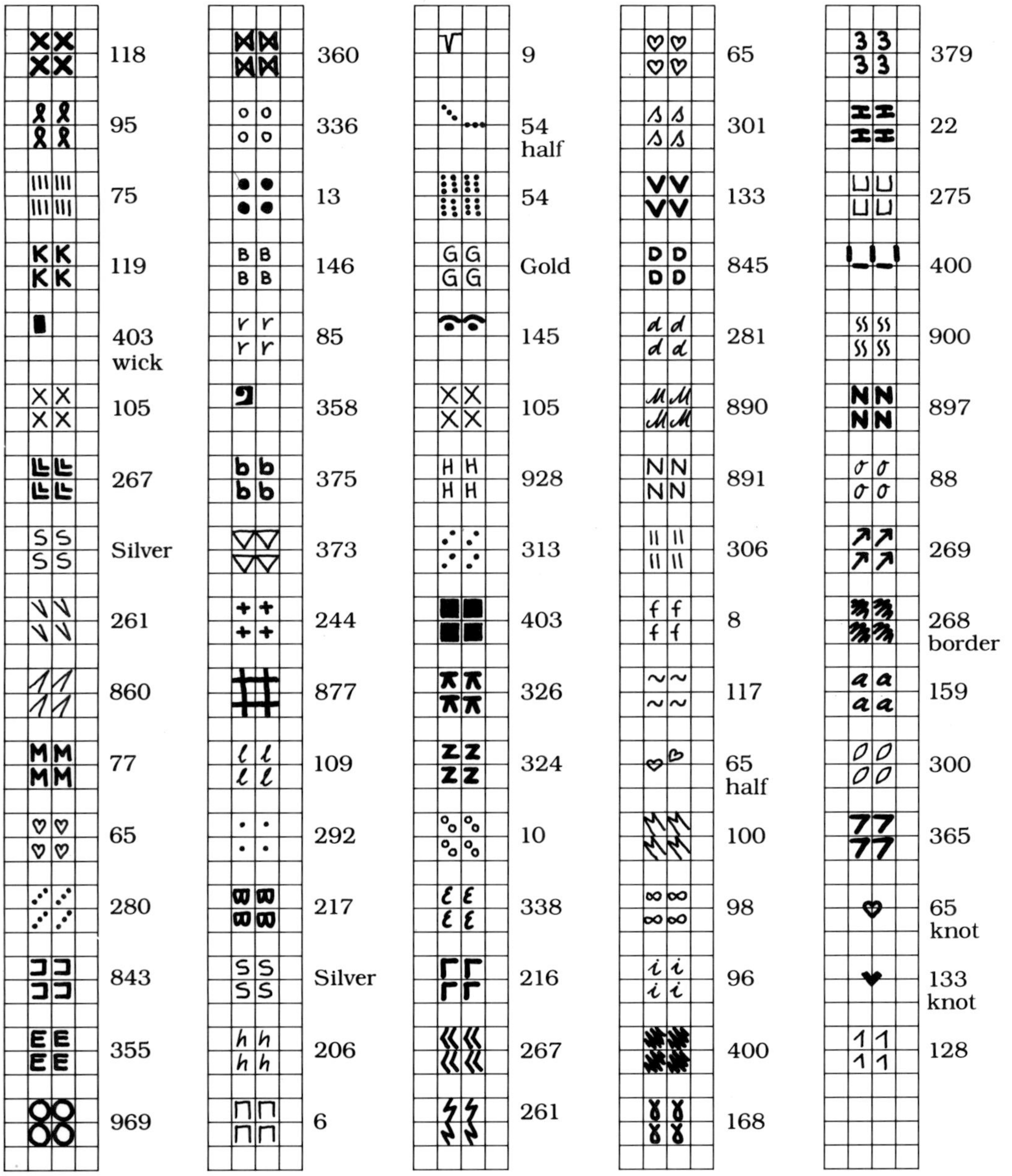

FROHE
WEIHNACHTEN
MERRY
CHRISTMAS
JOYEUX
NOEL
GOD
JUL
BOAS
FESTAS
FELIZ
NAVIDAD
HYRÄÄ
JOULUA
PRETTIGE
KERSTDAGEN
BUON
NATALE
FELICES
PASCUASY

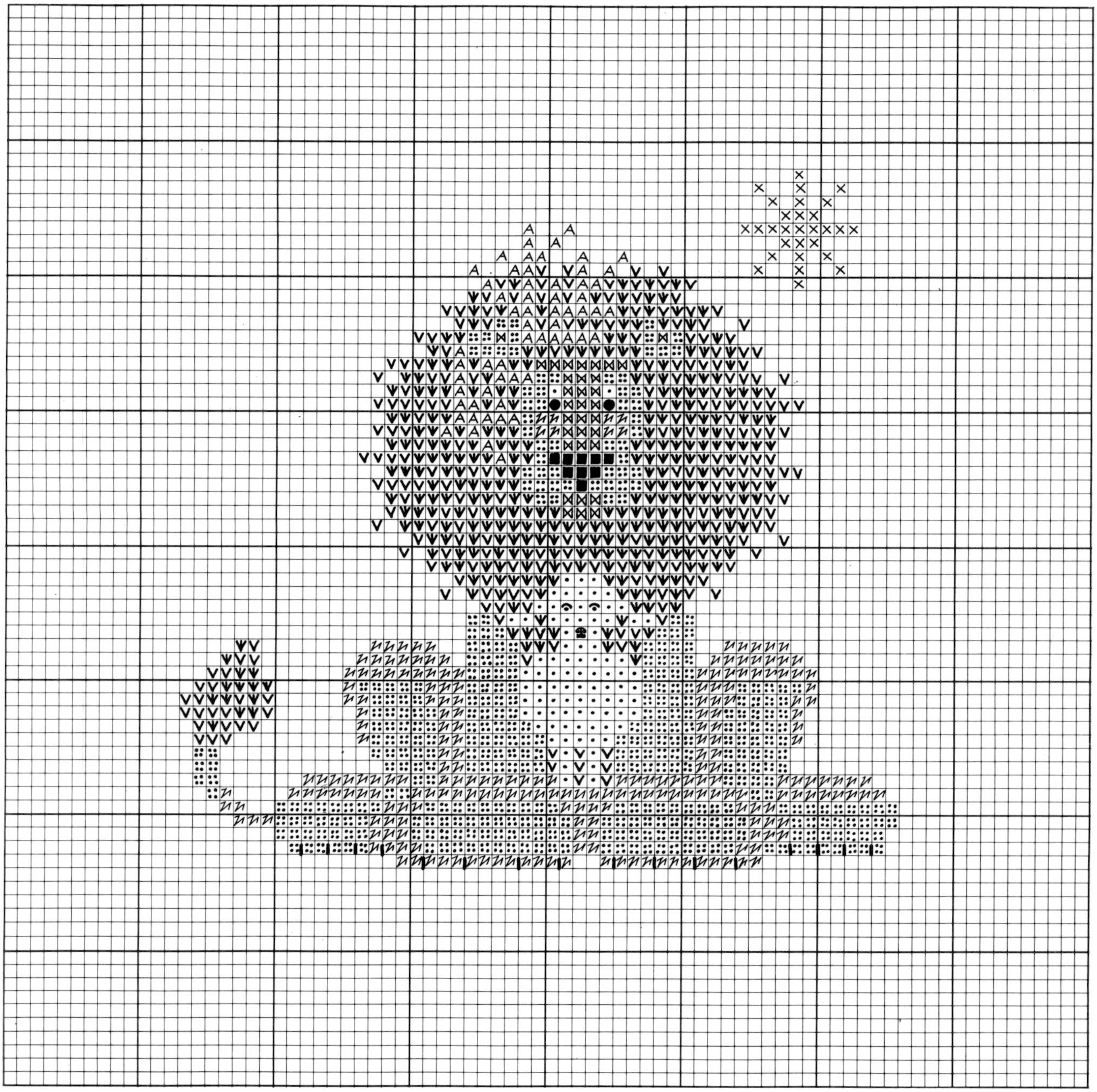

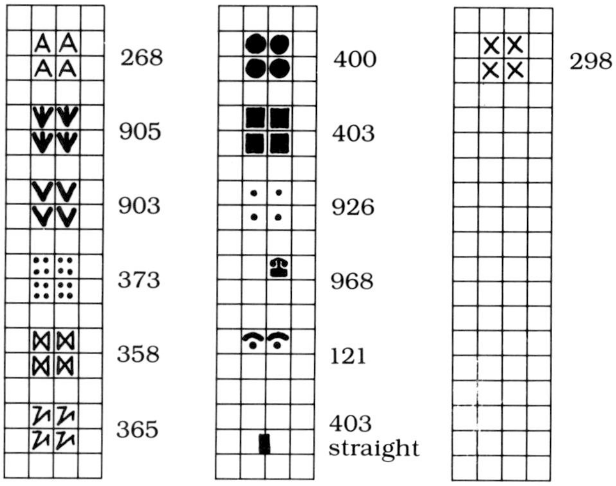
268
905
903
373
358
365
400
403
926
968
121
403 straight
298

The symbol of the lion and the lamb: a sampler that expresses our hope for peace. (Design: Katja Mackens Hassler.)

Size: 3¾ × 3¾ inches (9.5 × 9.5cm)

Time: appr. 6 hours

127
968
35
half
50
145
146
188
900
290
279
28
400
397
267
268
846
313
118
324
403
wick
Gold
Silver
35
98
112
298
290
65
88
46
928
22
847
403
372
375
360
168
10
9
365
120
940
970
54

Memories of Christmas past are awakened with this Christmas tree decorated in full splendor. And everybody will find a present among the many left under the tree!

Size: 6⅜ × 4½ inches (16 × 11.5cm)

Time: 15 hours

INDEX

aida cloth, 8
angels, 8, 13, 16–17, 37, 38–39, 53, 55, 57

bells, 38–39
birds, 15, 16–17, 33
borders, 6, 16–17
bows, 23, 27, 29, 33, 39, 47, 51, 53

candles, 13, 16–17, 38–39, 53, 55, 57, 63
carolers, 49

dogs, 35, 49

floss, embroidery, 6, 7, 10, 11

hearts, 13, 16–17, 23, 25, 31, 37, 44, 51, 57
horizontal rows, 5, 6

lamb, 61
linen, 8, 9
lion, 61

patterns, 7, 12, 14, 18–21, 22, 24, 26, 28, 30, 32, 34, 36, 40–41, 44–45, 46, 48, 50, 52, 54, 58–59, 60, 62
presents, 13, 35, 38–39, 44, 45, 47, 53, 63

Santa Claus, 13, 16–17, 38–39, 42–43, 47
size, estimating, 8
sled, 42–43, 53
stars, 13, 16–17, 35, 55, 63
Styrofoam, 6
symbols, 6, 12–13, 14, 15, 16, 22, 24, 26, 28, 30, 32, 34, 36, 38, 44, 46, 48, 50, 51, 54, 56, 60, 62

techniques for cross-stitch, 5, 6, 7,
teddy bear, 13, 31, 47, 57
topstitch, 5, 6, 7
trees, 13, 17, 31, 33, 37, 44, 47, 55, 57, 63

understitch, 5, 6

vertical rows, 5, 6

wreaths, 7, 16–17, 23, 25, 27, 29, 31, 39, 53